The
Painted
Wall

The Painted Wall

Transforming Your Walls with Stunningly Simple Paint Effects

Sacha Cohen

CREATIVE
PUBLISHING
international

CHANHASSEN, MINNESOTA

www.creativepub.com

First published in the USA and Canada in 2001 by
Creative Publishing International, Inc.

President/CEO: Michael Eleftheriou
Vice President/Publisher: Linda Ball
Vice President/Retail Sales & Marketing:
Kevin Haas
Executive Editor/Lifestyles: Elaine Perry

ISBN 0-86573-490-9

QUAR.TPW

Conceived, designed, and produced by
Quarto Publishing plc
The Old Brewery
6 Blundell Street
London
N7 9BH

Editor Kate Michell
Art Editor Sally Bond
Assistant Art Director Penny Cobb
Text Editors Claire Waite, Gillian Kemp
Designer Julie Francis
Photographers Paul Forrester, Colin Bowling
Picture Researcher Laurent Boubounelle
Indexer Dorothy Frame

Art Director Moira Clinch
Publisher Piers Spence

Manufactured in China by Regent Publishing
Services, Ltd
Printed in China by Midas Printing Limited

9 8 7 6 5 4 3

Contents

Introduction **6**

Preparation & Finishing Techniques **8**

off-white •
cream • stone
24

lemon • yellow
ocher • orange
38

smooth and soft
suedes
26

wallpaper
patterns
40

stone walls
30

multi-toned
colorwash
44

Organic Spectrum
34

stamped mosaic
48

Golden Hues
52

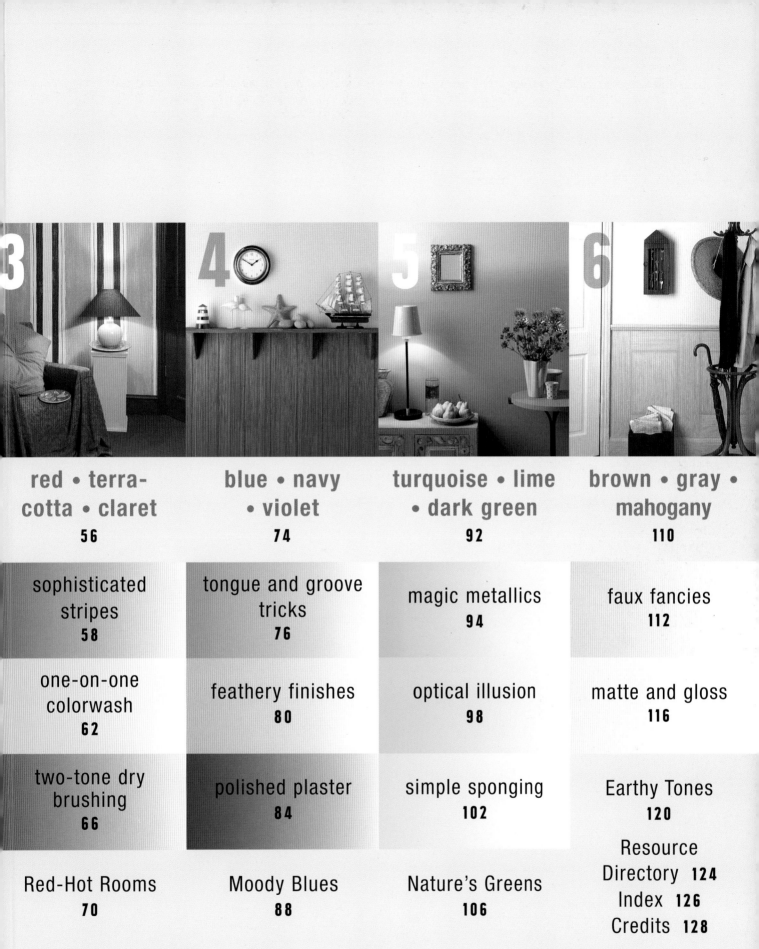

3

red • terra-cotta • claret
56

sophisticated stripes
58

one-on-one colorwash
62

two-tone dry brushing
66

Red-Hot Rooms
70

4

blue • navy • violet
74

tongue and groove tricks
76

feathery finishes
80

polished plaster
84

Moody Blues
88

5

turquoise • lime • dark green
92

magic metallics
94

optical illusion
98

simple sponging
102

Nature's Greens
106

6

brown • gray • mahogany
110

faux fancies
112

matte and gloss
116

Earthy Tones
120

Resource Directory **124**
Index **126**
Credits **128**

Introduction

The wall is the largest backdrop in any room, so the vast variety of ways to "dress" this area becomes an integral element in all room schemes. Venturing up the avenue of paint effects, armed with the huge breadth of paint colors now available, you will discover an endless palette from which any surface can be imitated, and the wall becomes a blank canvas for the imagination.

There are two options for any wall—either it becomes a coordinated backdrop to other strong elements within the room, such as furniture, bringing a scheme together; or the wall becomes the main feature in itself. The latter option is particularly useful when you don't have an abundance of paintings to hang on your wall, because the wall itself becomes the artwork.

The Painted Wall illustrates a broad spectrum of techniques for decorating your walls, all color coordinated for easy room scheming, and takes the reader through each process, from preparation to the finished makeover. The techniques illustrate a range of effects from imitating "real" surfaces, such as sandstone or mosaic tiling, to mood effects created by broken color work such as colorwashing or ragging. This book is approached with the opinion that any style, mood, or surface can be recreated with the simple use of paint.

The first section of the book runs through an easy-to-follow guide to the preparatory work that comes before the paint effect, with explanatory lists of basic tools, brushes, and paints. While color choice will always remain a matter of personal choice, the general principles involved in dealing with color are discussed, including particular consideration given to existing architectural elements. A certain amount of personal judgment will be needed in interpreting a scheme to a particular room, considering

◀ All the techniques described and illustrated in the following projects are quick and simple to learn, so before you know it you will be an expert.

◀ When applying a natural-look finish to your walls it is best to accessorize the room with organic materials such as wood. This will emphasize the back-to-basics feel you are attempting to create.

the available size, height, light, and proposed function of the area, but this section can at least guide you in the right direction.

The project section of the book is presented in six color coordinated chapters, featuring specific palettes that run concurrently with the color wheel: off-whites, with their pale, natural feel; lemon, yellow ocher to orange, with their bright, sunny tones; terra-cotta, red to claret, evoke rich, warm moods; blue, navy to violet, can be both soft and formal; turquoise, lime to dark green, for sharp, vibrant tones; and brown, gray to mahogany, as the new neutrals. Since the first step in redecoration often begins with the choice of the overall color, the aim has been to illustrate exactly which effects suit individual tastes and color palettes.

All the effects use basic matte latex paint as the main ingredient. The paint can be used in solid form, or diluted to make a "wash." This paint, whether solid or diluted, holds a good level of durability for the everyday wear and tear that a wall is likely to receive. With this paint there are no limits to the range of patterns, textures, and effects that can be created.

The Painted Wall acts as a sourcebook of effects and styles available within any color choice. The step-by-step guides explain how to recreate each look without the need for specialist knowledge or equipment, along with general advice and tips on problems that may occur. For further variety, alternative swatches of effects and colorways are offered to illustrate the choice of colors and techniques that can become a springboard for the creation of the perfect room. There is something for everyone, so be confident, be bold, roll up your sleeves, and get painting!

▲ If the idea of applying a paint effect to a whole wall is too daunting, build in a shelf or dado rail to act as a dividing line and then apply the technique to just above or below, and paint the rest of the wall in a complementary color.

◀ The placement of a striking decoration, such as this ornate framed mirror, will draw attention toward a specific area of the wall.

▶ Ordinary household items, such as synthetic sponges, can be used to transform your plain, flat walls into something far more interesting to the eye.

▲ Blue is believed to soothe and calm the mind according to color theory. It is, therefore, particularly suitable for bedrooms. It is always worth taking some time to contemplate the effect that colors can have on your mood before you finalize your paint color choice.

Planning a room scheme can be tackled in various ways and by taking some general elements into consideration. Taking time at this stage will save effort and regret further down the line.

Initial Planning

The first thing to consider is the amount of natural light the room receives, as this will have a great impact on color choices. The same color under an electric light can look quite different in a sun-filled room. Therefore, when choosing colors, try a little on each wall to see how they react in different lights at different times of the day. Then consider the type of atmosphere you would like to create—this might be bound to the function of the room; a formal dining room is quite different to a cozy sitting room, for example. Look at the existing features of the room, such as the fireplace or window. Are they modern, traditional, plain, or ornate? These are boundaries that will need to be worked around, unless, of course, you have a substantial budget and can change or remove existing elements to suit your style choice.

Looking through interiors magazines can be a good way of establishing the sort of look you require. First, make sure the room in question will lend itself to a similar scheme; attempting a grand baroque dining room in a small terraced house is mostly doomed from the outset. Then, break down the elements within the magazine images you like in order to get an idea of how to recreate the same look.

Another good approach is to find a fabric that you like and take your inspiration for the room from there. Choose your wall colors straight from the fabric, they may come from just a small detail in the pattern but at least you can see the colors working together.

◀ Always remember to take the features of a room into consideration when choosing a paint effect and color. This warm, yet bold, red particularly suits the dark, period fireplace.

▼ If you decide to apply a patterned paint effect to a room, make sure that it is going to create the right sort of atmosphere for that environment—for example, a delicate pattern is better suited to a bedroom or a nursery than a kitchen.

◀ If you have a particular fabric that you like, take it along to a hardware store to match it to color swatches of paints. You are almost certain to find the exact match considering the vast array of paints now available.

Paint effects use two or more colors to create certain moods or looks and reduce the need for expensive items to pull a style together. A large loose colorwash generally gives a relaxed, easy feel to a room, whereas a tight, structured wallpaper pattern will evoke a strict formality.

Obviously there are no hard and fast rules, only guidelines with hundreds of variables. If the final result is not successful, work out why and learn from it; after all, it only needs a repaint, two days' work at the most.

To start any decorating job, you need a basic kit of tools and equipment. This can be slowly expanded to include more specialized equipment as you develop your repertoire of paint effects.

Basic Equipment

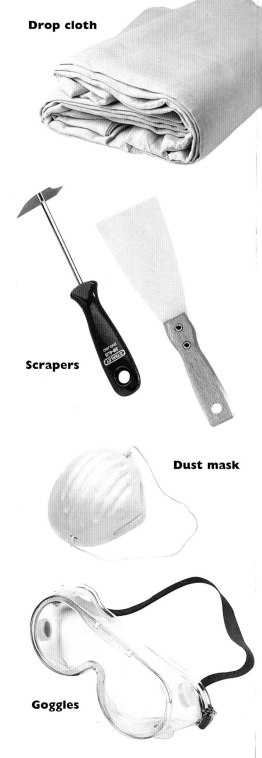

Drop cloth

Scrapers

Dust mask

Goggles

Ladders

A set of ladders should give you enough height to reach ceilings easily without stretching. Over-reaching makes the job more difficult and can be very dangerous. It is also important that the floor area is dry and level in order to prevent ladders from wobbling or slipping.

Drop cloths

Drop cloths should cover the floor area and any furniture that is too large or awkward to take out of the room. Cotton twill drop cloths are reusable and commonly available. These will prevent damage from roller spray or the odd drip, but since they are fabric they will not withstand a major spill. For a waterproof version use disposable plastic drop cloths, which provide complete protection.

Dust masks

Dust masks are essential when sanding, as the fine particles created can be a health hazard. Goggles are also useful.

Sandpaper

Sandpaper is available in a range of grades: fine, medium, coarse, and wet-dry. As all surfaces should be sanded to provide a key, choosing the right grade of paper for the job is essential and affects the standard of the final finish; for example, use a heavy or medium grade (depending on the condition of the wall) to clean up a previously painted wall, and a fine grade to smooth a filled hole. A sanding block provides an easy tool for sanding flat surfaces, allowing you to apply an even pressure over a large area.

Scrapers

Scrapers have various uses, from removing old flaking paint and stripping woodwork to doubling as a filling knife, but remember to clean the scraper thoroughly after using it for filling work.

Screwdrivers

Screwdrivers will be handy for removing door hard-ware and wall fixings, as well as opening paint cans. A multifunctional screwdriver with detachable heads will be of most use and covers all possibilities.

Paintbrushes

Household paintbrushes come in a variety of sizes and qualities. To compile a good basic set, aim at the middle of the range, not the cheapest. The better the standard of the brush the better the finish will be. A 1″ (25mm) and a 2″ (50mm) paintbrush will be sufficient for general painting, edges, and woodwork. A 4″ (100mm) brush is used as an alternative to a roller on the wall, and can

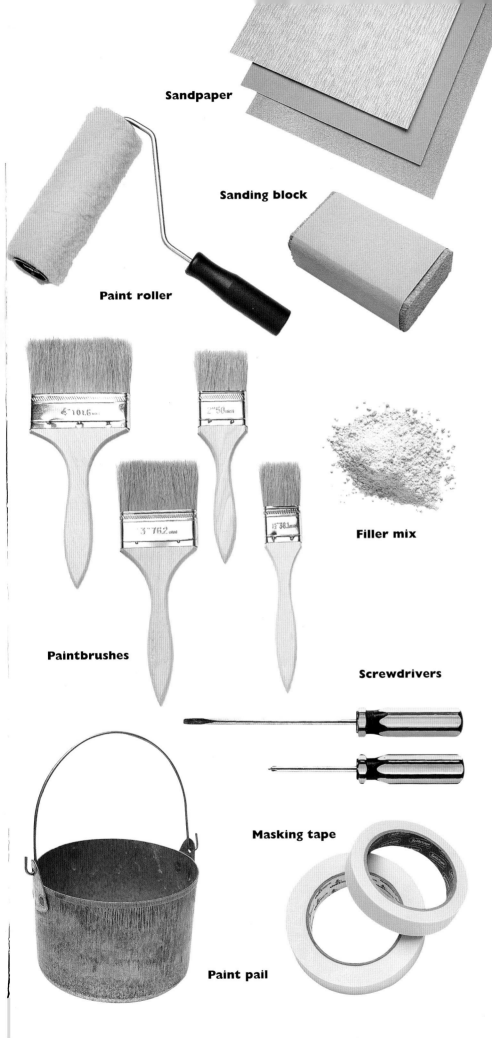

Sandpaper

Sanding block

Paint roller

Paintbrushes

Filler mix

Screwdrivers

Masking tape

Paint pail

also be used as a dusting brush. A ¼″ (6mm) artist's brush can be used to work into corners, narrow areas, and around fixtures and fittings.

Fillers

Interior wall and wood fillers are essential for the repair of any pitted areas or fine cracks in the walls or woodwork. They are applied with a scraper or filling knife and then sanded when dry to provide a smooth surface for the paint.

Paint pails

Paint pails are available in metal and plastic and sometimes with airtight lids for the storage of custom mixed colors or glazes. It is sensible to pour small quantities of paint from the main can into a pail, as it is lighter to hold and limits the damage caused by any spillage.

Paint roller

A paint roller provides the quickest application of paint over a large area. Buying a good quality natural roller sleeve will produce a smooth finish and avoid the potential "orange peel" effect created by cheaper, manmade rollers. Rollers usually come with roller trays, which provide a well for the paint and a flat surface to remove excess paint on. To paint the upper sections of the wall and ceiling, attach the roller to an extension pole, reducing the use of ladders and enabling quicker coverage.

Masking tape

Masking tape is available in various widths and levels of adhesion. A roll of 1″ (25mm) tape will cover most jobs, such as masking light fixtures and sockets and obtaining a clean edge along a baseboard.

A number of specialty paintbrushes have been designed to create particular effects with paints and washes. Remember that each effect you try will only use one or two of these brushes, so don't feel that you have to buy them all.

Specialty Brushes

Softening brushes

Softening brushes are traditionally made of expensive badger hair, but synthetic varieties are now available. They are generally used for blending and softening brush marks when creating faux finishes, such as marbling or wood graining. A good, cheap alternative is to use a large blusher brush.

Stencil brushes

Stencil brushes are round with a flat top that creates an even distribution of paint when stippling (dabbing paint on or off with the flat of the brush). Brushes sold specifically for stenciling tend to be quite expensive, but you can use any household paintbrush of a similar shape. Fitch brushes, which are usually used for painting small areas and edges, are also a good alternative to specialty stencil brushes; they are usually quite large, but you should only use the tip of the brush.

Dragging brushes

Dragging brushes have long bristles, which lie on a wide, flat handle. Flattening the bristles through a wash produces a dragged, stripy effect. A coarse household paintbrush can also produce adequate dragging marks.

Lining brushes

Lining brushes, or coachliners, have very long, thin bristles that hold a generous amount of paint, preventing the production of stop and start marks on a continuous line. They also paint a good, even line.

Stippling brushes

Stippling brushes or stippling blocks are larger versions of the stencil brush, with short, cut bristles that make fine, pinpoint marks in the painted surface. Again, they can be expensive, but a wallpaper pasting brush produces a very similar effect.

Swordliner

A swordliner is an angle-cut artist's brush only really used for veining when producing a marble effect. The handle should be held loosely, and the shape of the bristles produces a good vein. An alternative, which is equally easy to use and will give the same effect, is a large feather.

Fitch brushes

Coach liners

Stippling block

Sword liner

Softening brush

Stencil brushes

2" DRAGGER 32058 UK

Dragging brush

Cleaning

■ Brushes should always be cleaned immediately after use. New brushes should be washed before use to allow any loose bristles to "shed," otherwise you will find them sticking to the painted surface.

■ Brushes used with oil- or water-based paints demand different methods of cleaning.

■ If, when using oil-based paint, the same color and brush are going to be used again soon, store the brush in a jar of water; this prevents the paint from drying, keeping it suspended in the bristles.

■ To clean a brush used for oil-based paint properly after use, rinse it out well in a pail using

mineral spirits, until as much of the color is removed as possible. Then wash the brush in warm water using lots of dishwashing liquid until all the paint and mineral spirits have washed away.

■ When cleaning off water-based paints, wash with warm water and dishwashing liquid. If the paint has dried on areas of the bristles use a small nailbrush to remove it.

■ After washing all brushes, smooth out the hair and stand them in a container with the bristles upright, to dry and store.

Some extra items of equipment are required only for specific techniques, such as measuring and marking tools for creating repeat patterns, or foam rubber for making stamps.

Craft knife

Useful Extras

Plumbline

A plumbline can be bought or made—a weight at the end of some cord or string is used to establish a true vertical line. A bunch of keys on some twine acts just as well as a commercial line.

Tape measure

A tape measure is a general purpose item used when positioning patterns and stripes. It is more useful than a ruler since it can be placed in the tightest of corners.

Carpenter's level

A carpenter's level enables you to establish accurate horizontal and vertical lines. Measuring such lines from the floor or ceiling is not always accurate since some rooms, especially in older houses, have floors or ceilings that are not level.

Pencil

A pencil, preferably a hard version, should be used to make a faint mark to guide a wall pattern. Chalk is often used but can be difficult to see and less accurate because it is not as sharp.

Rubber decorating combs

Rubber decorating combs either have teeth that are graded in width, for use in wood-graining techniques, or have teeth of equal widths, but available in varying

sizes—often a triangular comb has teeth of different sizes on each of its three edges. Homemade combs can be customized from thick card but do not last indefinitely.

Craft knife

A craft knife is invaluable for cutting stencils, stamps, and templates, and should always be used with a new, sharp blade and pointing away from the body.

Paint pad

A paint pad is made of short pile on a sponge backing attached to a handle. Used as an alternative to a roller, with much less mess, it provides a flatter finish. It is also the best tool for creating perfectly edged stripes.

Natural sponges

Natural sponges are not only used for sponging, but also for colorwashing and mottling (see pages 30–33 and 102–105). Alternatively, pinch away at the top surface of a basic synthetic sponge, removing small chunks, to imitate the pitted look of a natural sponge.

Plumbline

Tape measure

Carpenter's level

Pencils

Rubber decorating combs

Paint pads

Masonry roller

Natural sponge

Chamois ragging leather

Foam rubber

Upholstery foam

Stencil card

Chamois leather

Chamois leather is the perfect material for ragging because even marks are easily achieved whether ragging paint on or off, as long as the cloth is refolded often (see pages 26–29).

Masonry roller

A masonry roller is used when painting very uneven surfaces. Its long pile forces the paint into cracks and pitted areas, while its shape and texture provide the perfect tool for roller fidgeting (see page 54).

Foam rubber

High-density foam rubber is the perfect material for making your own stamps and can be bought in small pieces as offcuts at foam specialty stores or art supply stores. Detailed patterns can be cut and will remain strong due to the thickness of the rubber. Synthetic foam such as upholstery foam can also be used, but only for simple designs since it does not cut as sharply as high-density foam rubber.

Stencil card

Stencil card is a waxed card that can be cut to any design and will not become too wet with the application of paint. Plastic folders or acetate are good alternatives, and folders will produce two stencils when cut. Acetate and plastic must be taped down flat for cutting, however, since the plastic tends to slip.

There is a huge range of paints and washes available in local hardware stores and from specialty paint suppliers. The following information should help you to choose the product you need.

Paints

As a general rule, only water-based paints should be used on walls. If oil-based paint were to be used this would probably have to be stripped, or at least well sanded, before it could be repainted, as the next coat simply will not stick and the plaster beneath cannot breathe. Oil-based paints are used for woodwork, making these much-used areas washable and highly durable. Certain paints can be used to protect areas of wall that are subject to damage from the backs of chairs, door openings, and so on; although this is often solved with the addition of a dado rail painted with a latex paint that can be wiped clean (see table). However, if the wall is going to receive excessive damage, a thin coat of an acrylic varnish will provide a more durable surface but will need to be sanded before repainting.

Always mix paint thoroughly, then pour it into a paint pail or a roller tray. Wipe the edge of the can and replace the lid securely. When you are working on a ladder use a hook to hang the pail from, so that you always have one hand free to hold on.

Health and Safety

- It is essential that you read and follow the manufacturer's instructions carefully on all products before starting work.

- Always work in a well-ventilated area.

- When using oil- and alcohol-based products wear rubber gloves to avoid skin contact.

- When using water-based products, avoid lengthy exposure to the skin to prevent irritation or drying out. Wear protective gloves if you have sensitive skin.

- When sanding or using toxic products, wear a dust mask and goggles to protect the eyes and lungs.

- Do not throw rags soaked with volatile liquid substances directly into the dustbin, but lay them out flat to dry before discarding.

- Always keep a bucket of water handy in case of accidents or splashes to the skin or eyes.

- Take care and time, since accidents often happen when you are rushed.

Paint	Base	To Dilute	Uses	Notes
Matte latex paint	Water	Water, wallpaper paste, acrylic glaze, acrylic varnish	Used in nearly all flat-color painting and paint effects	Fast drying, flat finish but can mark, wide color range
Satin latex paint	Water	Water, wallpaper paste, acrylic glaze, acrylic varnish	Used as matte latex paint, good base for paint effects	Fast drying, faint sheen finish, durable for bathrooms and kitchens, shows up imperfections, wide color range
Soft sheen latex paint	Water	Water, wallpaper paste, acrylic glaze, acrylic varnish	Too syrupy to use as a wash for paint effects, but makes a good base	Fast drying, mid-sheen finish, durable for bathroom and kitchen paint effects, shows up imperfections, wide color range
Masonry paint (sand textured)	Water	Not to be diluted	Creating texture	Sand textured so can be rough, limited color range
Colorwash	Water	Already diluted	Ready-mixed wash for broken color work	Expensive, translucent, limited color range
Stencil paint	Water	Not to be diluted	Stenciling, stamping, and freehand painting	Flat finish, small pots, wide color range
Artist's acrylic paint	Water	Water, wallpaper paste, acrylic glaze, acrylic varnish	Tinting any water-based paint, making washes, stenciling	Flat finish, strong, pigments inexpensive, wide color range
Universal tint	Water	Water, wallpaper paste, acrylic glaze, acrylic varnish	Tinting	Strong pigments, wide color range
Milk paint	Water	Water, wallpaper paste, acrylic glaze, acrylic varnish	Basic large wall areas	Dense, matte finish, moderate color range
Powder paint	Water	Water, wallpaper paste, acrylic glaze, acrylic varnish	Tinting, making washes	Gritty, needs a binder (gum arabic), limited color range
Impasto	Water	Not to be diluted	Thick paint for textured effects	Can be tinted with universal tint, hard work

The end result of any paint effect will depend on the initial preparation of the surface. This stage of decoration is always tedious, but pays off once the painting has begun. Taking shortcuts will stand out and could ruin the final concept.

Preparation

Remove as much of the room's contents as possible: this will make the job quicker and easier since you have the space to move freely around, resulting in fewer accidents. Cover the whole floor area with drop cloths to prevent any damage, taping them with masking tape to the baseboard for complete coverage.

Any old flaking paint or wallpaper must be removed before you redecorate, and the surface should be cleaned and sanded. Any cracks or holes should be filled with interior wall filler and a filling knife, then sanded smooth when dry. If

◀ For certain paint finishes it is essential that the walls are completely smooth. Repair any cracks or dents in your walls with filler. It is easier to apply filler to large cracks with a trowel, whereas smaller cracks or dents should be filled using a more delicate filling knife.

the walls are quite badly damaged, hang a heavy grade of lining paper which should smooth over any major problems.

Starting with a coat of white latex paint is a cheap way of priming the walls before the next coats and effects are applied. New plaster will need a "mist" coat for priming; this involves diluting latex paint (again use white for economy) with an equal amount of water and brushing or rolling it on. The "mist" will soak into the plaster, stopping the next coat from sitting on the surface like a skin, which is likely to peel in the future.

Textured surfaces will have to be flattened before attempting

◀ Freshly plastered walls will absorb water very easily, therefore it is important to prime them with a dilute wash of latex paint. Mix equal amounts of paint and water in a paint pail to achieve the correct wash consistency.

▶ Protect the edges of light switches, moldings, and any other wall fixtures with masking tape; this is easily removable and leaves no marks.

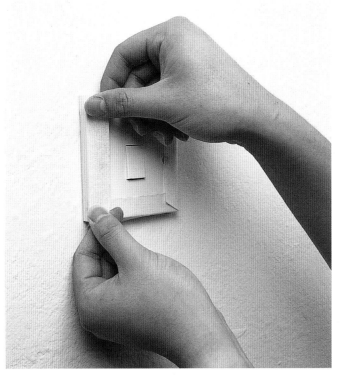

Start Painting

Always paint in a practical order; ceiling, walls, then woodwork.

Start with the large areas of the ceiling and walls, using an extension pole for the roller where necessary. Load the roller well but make sure it's not dripping or uneven. Roll out the paint for a smooth, even finish, but do apply a generous coat for good coverage of color.

Then paint the edges and corners in with a brush, filling in the gaps where the roller couldn't reach and providing clean, straight edges. The paint should never cover more than two-thirds of the bristles of the brush, keeping the handle clean and the paint in control.

When the first flat coat has dried, you can get to the fun part of applying the special effects.

any paint effect. Unfortunately, this usually involves skimming plaster over the top of the previous pattern to create a smooth surface.

Carefully mask all light switches and light fittings, sockets, and the baseboard with masking tape, making sure the tape is straight and pressed down firmly. This should be removed as soon as the

painting is done, even when still wet, because the longer the tape is on the more residue will be left on the surface.

Arrange all the necessary paints and equipment in the center of the room and try to keep them as neat and clean as possible. This sense of tidiness will stop the effects from becoming sloppy and make the job easier for you.

◀ ▶ Always transfer paint to a paint pail to lessen the chances of major spills; the edge of a paint pail is also a good place to brush excess paint off your brush. Remember never to load your brush with paint any further than three-quarters of the way up the bristles.

Paint effects are created using either undiluted paint straight from the container, or using diluted paint mixtures, known as washes, for broken color work.

Paint Effects

Making and Using Washes

A wash is simply made from diluted paint, a mixture that allows you to work the desired marks into it using brushes, cloths, or other tools. The mixture remains wet longer than undiluted paint, therefore giving you more time to work the surface and reduce the creation of "joins" between paint patches.

Wallpaper paste is a good, cheap binder for making washes as it retards the drying time but also provides a thick, controllable mixture. The general ratio for a wash is 50 percent paint to 50 percent wallpaper paste, although you can make a more translucent wash by using more wallpaper paste to paint. Water and acrylic varnish can also be used, and acrylic glaze (which is a more expensive binder) is designed specifically for making washes. "Colorwash" is a ready-colored, ready-diluted mixture, also specifically for washes.

With any binders or ready-made washes, time is always of the essence. Prepare everything before you start applying, so there is no need to stop once a section has been started. Only break from one corner to the next. Always begin in a top corner, alternating between working the next area downward then across.

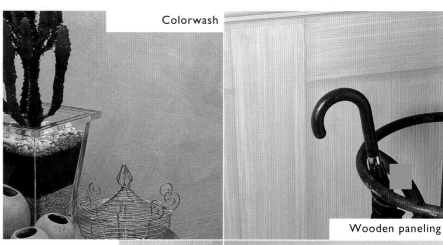

Colorwash

Wooden paneling

Rag rolling

Grading

Effects Using Washes

Antiquing	Fossilstone marble	Polished plaster
Basketweave	Frottage	Rag rolling
Chenille	Grading	Stippling
Clay wall	Layered ragging	Stone blocking
Clouding	Leather	Wall art
Colorwash	Marbling	Wall panels
Damask	Mother of pearl	Wooden paneling
Denim	Mottled colorwash	
Dragging	Mottling	

The most important part of a wash is its consistency. This will be the greatest variable in the finished effect. Deciding how thick or thin, how opaque or translucent you want the effect to be, will also depend on the color you are using, the base coat, and the desired effect.

Always make up more wash than is needed, because the same consistency can never be achieved twice. However, a wash will generally go a long way; in fact 4 pints (2.25l) will cover most rooms. Alternatively, you could use a measuring jug while mixing to record exact ingredients for reproducing the mixture.

A good undercoat for washes is a white satin finish. This will not change the tone of the base coat or top wash coat and provides a slippery surface that won't immediately absorb the two paint mixtures.

Choosing different colors for the base coat and the top wash coat is a tricky business since one will change the look of the other, maybe even creating a third. Practice is the only way of really knowing what to expect, so try out some color combinations on spare board before you tackle the walls. However, there are a few general points to remember with regard to color. A darker color over a lighter one will create a rich finish with depth, while the reverse will appear more muted and chalky. The stronger the difference in tone or color between the base and top coats, the greater the effect. If using a white base coat make sure the top wash coat is not a strong tone, since then a perfect execution of the effect will become vitally important, as the base coat will easily show through where the effect is not even.

Layering many colors can create a great sense of depth and interesting results. But when using latex paint washes note that they can be quite opaque, so try to keep the consistency thin so that each color is not totally obscured.

Hand-painted stripes

Sponging

Stamped mosaic

Stenciling

Effects Using Undiluted Paint

Aged paint	Layered sponging	Stamped wallpaper
Borders	Matte and gloss	Stenciling
Crackle glaze	Moorish tiles	Stripes
Cricket stripes	Roller fidgeting	Rubber floor
Distressing	Sky	
Dry brushing	Sponging	
Feather print	Squares	
Hand-painted stripes	Stamped mosaic	

Color is ultimately a matter of personal opinion, and colors can evoke all sorts of moods, emotions, and memories. With color, there are no right or wrongs, but there are some general guidelines to aid your choice.

Color

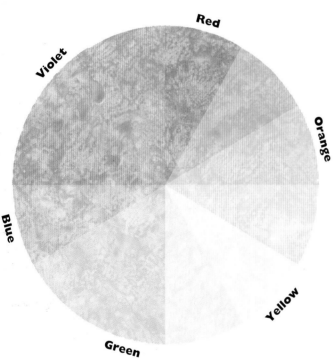

The color wheel illustrates the generally accepted rules of color. There are 12 colors falling into three categories, starting with the three key primary colors; red, yellow, and blue. All other colors are mixed from differing proportions of these primary colors. The three secondary colors are obtained by mixing two of the primaries in equal quantities; orange (red and yellow), green (blue and yellow), and violet (blue and red). Finally, there are six tertiary colors obtained by mixing each of the primary colors with its closest secondary: yellow and orange, orange and red, red and violet, violet and blue, blue and green, and green and yellow.

The pure colors of the color wheel are very intense and rarely applicable to a room scheme. Therefore, a "tone" of the color, whether lighter or darker, will prove easier to live with.

The amount of color used in the room can alter its mood or have a dramatic effect. A color used in large areas will create an overall atmosphere, while a color on small details will act as a highlight, emphasizing a feature or a tone of the main room color. An informed, clever use of color can appear to change

◄ Colors that are immediately opposite each other on the color wheel are termed complementary. For example, violet is complementary to yellow, as green is to red. These opposites mutually enhance each other and therefore appear more intense when used together.

◄ Contrasting colors are ones that have no similar base or opposites. Used together these can have a dramatic effect, but must be kept in the same tone.

◄ Colors that are near to each other on the color wheel are called harmonious. Having similar bases makes them work well together. For example, orange, yellow, and red; or red, violet, and blue.

◄ To attempt to describe primary colors as either warm or cold does not run true as a general rule. There are so many varying tones of each color that a violet-based blue can seem warm where as a green-based blue can appear cold.

visually the proportions of a room, mainly by the use of sectioning.

Traditionally, picture rails—about 24″ (600mm) from the ceiling—and/or dado rails—about 36″ (900mm) from the floor—section a room. How you fill in the gaps between these rails can emphasize the perspective within that room. For example, to make a ceiling feel lower, paint a dark color to the picture rail with a pale one from the rail over the ceiling. To make a room cozier, paint a dark tone below the dado rail with a warm tone from the dado rail up the walls and across the ceiling, thus enclosing the room.

Natural shades are easy on the eye and simple to incorporate into an interior. Synthetic colors can take a little bit of time and practice to use successfully and to avoid them looking plastic or too loud.

The use of texture with color can greatly alter that color's tone and the room's overall mood. Solid, glossy finishes are generally associated with working areas, efficiency, and durability. Layered chalky textures on the other hand give a sense of mellow depth and warmth to a room. This effect is also emphasized by the levels of light striking the wall finish, highlighting the technique

used. A broken, washed version of a color can also create a totally different mood to the solid version; for example, if a dark red is used as a colorwash over white, the broken color reveals all the tones used to make up the red, but this strong effect is weakened if you use the red wash over a color of the same tone, such as orange.

The only way to anticipate the look and feel of your chosen color scheme and paint effect, is to try it out on some spare board and position it in different parts of the room at different times of the day, to get a good idea of its effect under all circumstances.

▲ This light blue is an extremely clean and fresh color, and is, therefore, ideal for a bathroom.

◄ Warm up a room with bright colors, but by using these colors with a soft colorwash finish, a relaxed ambient feel is created.

off-white · cream · stone

The off-white palette ranges from nearly white to the deep hues of stone. These shades and tones coordinate well with each other and avoid color clashes. In technical terms they are all based on white, with the smallest touch of color within them. So a yellow-based cream would work well with other yellows, oranges, and reds, while a green-based stone color works with blues and greens.

The shades in this palette particularly suit those parts of the house with colorful vistas, so use them in a room that has a view of the ocean, or in one that looks out over the gray-blues of winter and the richer green tones of spring.

When choosing a neutral color scheme, think about texture as well as color, to keep the look interesting. Explore the patterns and feel of stone, of old limewashed walls, beaten sandy beaches, and the softness of wool, suede, and leather. Recreate these shades and textures in the home to produce a contemporary look.

Suede is a wonderfully luxurious material, and is very much the fabric of today, so to apply a suede effect to your walls is the ultimate in both opulence and fashion.

smooth and soft suedes

To achieve the suede effect, two layers of a colored wash are applied and ragged—dabbed with a folded cloth. The second layer softens the end result and disguises any joins in wash patches from the first ragged coat.

The key to creating this effect lies in using authentic looking suede colors—here warm buff over white produces the soft suede look. Use natural earth tones; matching a paint chart directly to a piece of suede will ensure an accurate color choice. If you want a darker effect, adjust the base color by tinting white with a little of the top coat, to avoid the difference between the two layers being too extreme.

The technique in itself imitates folded fabric and can be adjusted according to the thickness and type of cloth used. Thick cellulose cloths, as used here, or chamois leathers will create soft, large fold marks in the paint. For very tight marks, a thin cloth made from a material that is not too porous makes small folds and removes smaller amounts of wash, keeping the print marks sharp—unsuitable as a suede effect but, if used with a rich jewel color, it creates a unique crushed velvet look.

A specially made ragging roller can be used for speed, but a cloth that creates similar marks will be needed for edges and corners.

Groundwork Since this effect involves layering colored washes it will disguise any small cracks or dents in the wall, so it is not necessary to fill these. Large cracks or holes should be filled. Prepare the surface accordingly, following the instructions on pages 18–19.

1 The first wash Pour equal quantities of wallpaper paste and buff matte latex paint into a paint pail and mix together thoroughly. Take a 3″ (75mm) paintbrush and dip half the bristles into the wash. Scrape off the excess on the rim of the paint pail. Starting in the top corner of the wall, apply the wash to an area of a manageable size, such as a rough square of about 36″ (900mm). Stroke the mixture onto the wall in random directions.

MATERIALS AND TOOLS	
■ Warm buff matte latex paint	■ Thick cellulose cloth or chamois leather
■ Wallpaper paste	■ Paint pail
■ 3″ (75mm) paintbrush	

2 **Smooth it out** Immediately, using the same paintbrush, stipple all over the paint mixture in a pouncing motion to remove all traces of the previous brush strokes.

3 **Ragging** Again act quickly. Loosely fold a thick cellulose cloth or a chamois leather and dab it over the wet surface. This should create folds in the colored wash by removing the mixture where the cloth touches the surface. Alternate the angle of the cloth and refold it quite often, to give a varied, natural look that is not too regimented. Working quickly, brush the wash mixture onto the next 36" (900mm) area of the wall, working the wash just up to the previous patch, but not covering it. Use the same brush to stipple all over the wash to cover the previous brush strokes. Take care to seamlessly blend the two patches together by stippling the join. Immediately take the cloth and dab over the area as before, using a little extra pressure over the join. Continue over the whole wall, then leave to dry thoroughly.

4 **The second wash** The mixture used for the second layer should be slightly thinner than the first, otherwise the coverage will be too opaque. Use 1½ parts wallpaper paste to 1 part latex paint. Before you apply the first patch of the second wash layer, look carefully at the first layer and how the areas were worked. With the second layer you want to work in completely different patches, in order to disguise the joins from the first wash coat. Use the 3" (75mm) paintbrush and random brush strokes to apply an area of wash.

5 ▪ Keep it smooth
Use the same brush to stipple the wash and disguise the previous brush strokes.

6 More ragging Loosely fold the cloth as before and dab it over the wet wash to remove it in places. Frequently refold and change the angle of the cloth to produce a random, fluid finish. Following Step 3, continue covering the wall with patches of stippled and ragged wash. Leave to dry.

Trade secrets

▪ This effect needs to be done quickly, so it can be easier for two people to work at the same time. Always use the same person for brushing on while the other does the ragging, because, as with a signature, no two people will do an effect in exactly the same way. Using this method you will find that there are fewer, if any, joins in the wash, resulting in a professional looking finish.

Stone walls are perfect if you are trying to achieve a rustic look in your home, but the real thing can tend to be cold and dusty, so this imitation provides a warm, clean version of golden sandstone.

stone walls

This effect attempts to imitate the realistic appearance of a wall of sandstone blocks. So viewing the real thing will prove to be of great help when it comes to choosing the color and creating the effect. The real shades of sandstone range from pale cream to a deep yellow, so the tones you choose can be varied according to the depth of color suitable for the area being painted. Always use two quite contrasting tones, with the darker one making up the base coat.

Two different effects are used to build up the texture, sponging and dry brushing. The lighter top coat, applied sparingly and evened out with a dry brush, doesn't eliminate the base coat so a ghosting effect is created. One side of the "block" is then highlighted with a sponging technique. Note that the highlighted side should always be on the same side as the light source, usually the largest window in the room.

Groundwork Since this effect consists of rubbing the wall with paint on a sponge, any defects in the surface will be highlighted. However, because the technique aims to imitate sandstone in which cracks and dents occur naturally, these can enhance the overall effect, but will appear more dramatic than they really are. It is a matter of personal taste whether a strong look is required or a smoother, subtle finish would be more suitable. If the latter is preferable, all the cracks and dents will need to be filled and sanded. Prepare the surface accordingly, following the instructions on pages 18–19.

1 The base coat Pour some yellow ocher matte latex paint into a paint pail. Dip the front surface of the sponge into the paint, scrape the excess off on the edge of the pail, and rub the paint onto the wall in a circular motion.

MATERIALS AND TOOLS

- Yellow ocher matte latex paint
- Cream matte latex paint
- Biscuit matte latex paint
- Synthetic sponge
- 1" (25mm) paintbrush
- 4" (100mm) paintbrush
- Lining brush
- Paint pail
- 17 x 12" (430 x 300mm) card template
- Pencil

2 Laying off Pour cream matte latex paint into a clean paint pail. Dip the tips of a 4″ (100mm) paintbrush into the paint and scrape off any excess on the rim of the pail. Apply to the wall in random directions, holding the brush almost parallel to the surface.

3 The top coat Work in a manageable area of about 36″ (900mm) square. Make sure the paint is brushed out as far as possible, ensuring it is not too thick. Without adding more paint to the brush, go over the surface again to cover any obvious brush marks. Work in random directions with large sweeping strokes. Continue over the whole area, trying to keep the texture quite mottled, and without completely obliterating the base coat. Move on to an adjacent area and apply the paint in the same way, blending the edge of this patch with the edge of the first area using the dry brush. Leave to dry.

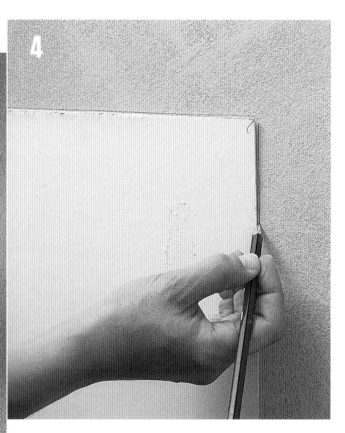

4 Roughing the blocks Take a rectangle of card, 17″ x 12″ (430mm x 300mm) to use as a template for the stone blocks. Starting at a bottom corner of the wall, use a pencil to draw lightly around the card template. Continue drawing blocks along the bottom of the wall, using the previous block as a positioning guide. Each stone block should be slightly uneven, to appear realistic. For the second row, stagger the blocks to form a brick pattern.

THE PAINTED WALL

5 Highlights Tear off a small chunk of the sponge. Dip it into the cream matte latex paint and scrape off as much paint as possible. Rub the sponge along the top and side edges of each block to form highlights and make each one individual. Then use the sponge to blend the paint out toward the middle. Continue until all the blocks are finished, varying the amount of paint sponged on each block. Leave to dry.

Trade secrets

■ A realistic "grout" look is enhanced if you arch the joins between some vertical and horizontal lines, to create slightly rounded corners. Keep these arcs small to give a subtle shadow effect, rather than large cement lines.

■ The only real skill needed in this effect is in the lining. A specialty brush will help immensely, not only in keeping the line straight, but also in the speed of painting. Coachliners are the traditional tools used by signwriters to obtain long, even lines whose width is determined by the size of brush used. They have extremely long, narrow hairs that allow the brush to hold a lot of paint while producing a consistent line. Coachliners can be tricky to get used to and you will need practice in controlling the long bristles. A good alternative is a lining brush, as used in this project; lining brushes have shorter bristles that hold less paint than coachliners, but are easier to control.

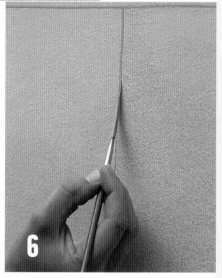

6 Lining Dilute some biscuit matte latex paint with water in a paint pail until it is the consistency of thin cream. Using a lining brush, carefully paint over all the pencil lines. Increasing the pressure on the brush will thicken the line, so vary the pressure used for a random, natural look.

Organic Spectrum

Drawing on the tones and hues of naturally occurring materials such as stone, marble, and shells there are a range of techniques that you can apply to create a whole array of rooms—from the light and airy feel of a pearlescent wash, to the contemporary style of a geometric border.

▲ Crackle glaze

The subtle use of an off-white crackle glaze (see page 73) in a period house enhances the antique feel of a room, and particularly suits a formal room, such as a dining room or library.

▼ Lime plaster

To create the traditional look of old, textured lime plaster, several layers of varying tones are dry brushed over each other (see pages 66–69). A warm beige base coat adds depth to the effect, while two top tones of lime and off-white build up the sense of texture. Leave a little of the beige base color visible when applying each layer. This is an effective technique to use on a poor, uneven wall area since it creates an allover texture that disguises the pitfalls of the present surface.

▲ Vertical stripes

There are several methods that can be used to create straight-edged bands of color. Marking the stripes with masking tape is quite time consuming, and the paint often bleeds underneath, or the tape removes some of the base paint when lifted. Another idea, using a roller to paint stripes, will give uneven edges that can be a feature in their own right. The easiest and quickest way to produce crisp lines is to use a paint pad, available in several widths. Only one line needs to be drawn to run the pad along. Here a pale stone base has had mid-stone stripes applied using an 8″ (200mm) paint pad.

▲ Trompe l'oeil

A trompe l'oeil effect (see pages 112–115) on an off-white wall recreates the look of sumptuous green/gray drapes, giving the impression that the real drapes continue around the bath. This technique is an effective way of using wall art to complement other features in a room.

▲ Simple stippling

On this example, the stippling technique—dabbing a special stippling brush over a wet wash to create small dotted marks—has been amended slightly: the brush used to apply the wash is also used to stipple it. Start with a solid, dark cream base coat, then mix together equal amounts of pure white matte latex paint and water or wallpaper paste. Brush the wash onto the wall using random brush strokes, then immediately stipple over the top in a pouncing motion. A standard household brush makes larger marks than a stippling brush and so produces a stronger effect. Be aware of any drips occurring—working from the top of the wall downward should prevent any great mishaps.

▲ Geometric border

A border like this can be drawn around the room without any measuring. Just judge the spacing by eye and draw in the lines with a carpenter's level. Start with a solid base coat of light beige, then use a mid-beige for the larger rectangles, followed by the darkest color, eggplant, that will easily cover all the paler colors. Use the eggplant shade on only the smallest rectangles, to avoid this stronger color becoming too dominant. A specialty pearlescent glaze completes the final layer of rectangles; this is a semi-translucent glaze that provides a range of tones when it overlaps the other colors already applied.

◀ Fossilstone marble

This effect must only be attempted on a completely smooth, flat, vertical surface that allows the paint colors to run together. Dilute pale beige matte latex paint with water to the consistency of thin cream. Dip a short-bristled brush into the diluted paint then spatter it—flick the handle of the brush to produce small spots of color on the surface. To cover a whole wall, first spatter with one color, then allow to dry before spattering the second shade, cream, in the same way. The colors will then remain defined. Alternatively, the effect can be carried out on flat panels that can be fixed to the wall. Spatter the first color until most of the white base is covered, then spatter the second shade while the first is still wet. Let the paint do the rest of the work by slightly running together but not completely mixing.

◀ Mother of pearl

A pearlescent wash—a specialty wash with a slight sheen and a pearl finish—is used to produce a mother of pearl effect. The base coat can vary from flat beige to salmon pink. If a real piece of mother of pearl is used as a reference, note the different shades that appear under the sheen. On this example, a pink wash was painted over a beige base coat, followed by a heavy coat of pearlescent wash. The pearlescent wash was stippled all over with a pouncing motion to disguise any brush marks. When dry, another pearlescent coat was applied and stippled as before.

▲ Basic antiquing

A simple antique wash will age and deepen any surface. The choice of base coat will have a great bearing on the final effect. To keep a light feel use a pale cream solid base coat. Heavily dilute some acrylic quick-drying woodstain— about 8 parts water to 2 parts woodstain—and lightly sponge the woodstain all over the surface. Watch out for any drips: these must be cleared away immediately using paper towels. This effect should highlight any existing pitted or cracked areas, while also adding a light brown staining to give a sense of natural aging.

lemon · yellow ocher · orange

The diverse selection of yellows, oranges, and ochers makes this a vibrant palette to work with. Think of the range of colors between buttercup yellow and earthy mustard, bright orange and raw sienna. Colors that are complementary to this palette are the obvious terra-cottas to deep reds, but this range also works well with contrasting hues such as blue or purple. It is a good idea, when combining yellows and oranges with other colors, to keep clean tones and colors together and, similarly, to keep the muted variations together.

Consider using this palette in a cool room that receives little sunlight. The warmth of the yellow and orange range can make a room feel welcoming, even when you thought it was too cold to be cozy. However, since these are generally bright colors, it is important to use them in subtle ways, for example as colorwashes or in simple dry brushing effects, rather than as a solid color, which would overpower any room, however bleak.

One way of getting unique wallpaper is not to trawl the department stores looking for something a little different, but to create your own wallpaper "look" with paint and stencils.

wallpaper patterns

This simple stencil technique allows repeat patterns to be quickly painted over the whole wall. A hand-painted feel is created by using only one guideline for positioning, so the pattern is naturally less accurate in places. A guideline can be drawn for every row if a more precise feel is required.

The stencil can be made from specialty waxed stencil card, or from plastic sheets or acetate, whichever is easy to get hold of. Cut the pattern of your choice out of the stencil using a craft knife. When using the stencil, remember to wipe it clean regularly to ensure that it will always lie flat against the wall.

The pattern used here is visually quite intense, so this effect is most suitable for use on a feature wall, such as a chimney breast or in alcoves, so that the whole effect doesn't become overpowering. Remember that it is best to paint the darker color, here a pale yellow, over the lighter, crisp white, for the best coverage.

Groundwork This is one effect where the surface of the wall must be perfect. If the stencil is painted over an uneven surface the pattern will distort, not only emphasizing the problem but also making the repeat pattern impossible to match up. This is an effect to be used on new plaster or heavy duty lining paper. Prepare the surface accordingly, following the instructions on pages 18–19.

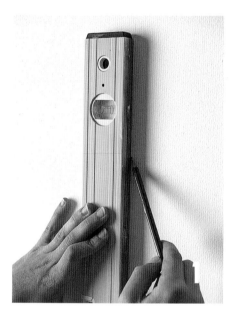

1 The base coat and guideline Apply two coats of white matte latex paint with a roller and leave to dry. This layer must be solid so if any ghosting occurs (normally when covering a very dark color) an extra coat may be needed. Using a carpenter's level, draw a vertical line in the middle of the wall to act as a positioning guide for the first stencil print.

MATERIALS AND TOOLS

- White matte latex paint
- Pale yellow matte latex paint
- Roller and tray
- Large fitch brush
- Small artist's brush
- Stencil
- Tape measure
- Pencil
- Carpenter's level
- Low-tack masking tape
- Damp cloth

2 **3**

4

2 Preparing the stencil
Tear off a length of low-tack masking tape about the size of the stencil width. Press the tape against your clothing to remove excess tack and lessen the chance of it removing any paint from the wall. Press the tape along the top of the stencil: this allows you to lift and check the print while painting without having to painstakingly reposition and realign the stencil by hand. Attach a length of tape in the same way to the bottom of the stencil. Find a part of the stencil that positions nicely over the pencil line and can be easily repeated, and press the tape in place.

3 Stenciling
Pour a little pale yellow matte latex paint into the well of a clean roller tray, keeping the paint contained and providing an area on the flat section of the tray for dabbing off excess paint. Dip the tips of a large fitch brush into the paint and dab off the excess. When stenciling always use the paint sparingly. Stencil the pattern by dabbing the flat of the brush over the surface in a pouncing motion. Add more paint when needed, but sparingly. Carefully roll the tape at the bottom of the stencil away from the wall. Lift the stencil while still fixed to the wall by the top line of tape, and check that it is evenly covered with paint. If necessary, replace the stencil and go over areas again.

4 The next print
Peel the stencil back and carefully roll the tape at the top away from wall. Reposition the stencil next to the first print, aligning it top and bottom with the previous print.

5 Continuing the line
Fill in the stencil with yellow paint as before. Use a damp cloth to wipe away the paint at the base and top edges of the stencil, so that you can see through the acetate to align it in the next position. Continue in the same way, following Steps 3–5, across the wall.

6 The next row To start on the row underneath, line up the top edge of the stencil pattern with the edge of the print above. Attach the stencil to the wall with tape.

7 Working to completion Continue by following Steps 3–5. Use the same techniques to line the stencil up in rows above and below the previous rows to complete the pattern across the whole wall. Leave to dry. Any smudges or bleeds can be touched up at the end using the base color and a small artist's brush.

Trade secrets

■ This technique is quite time consuming so, for quicker application, photocopy the design a few times, join up the motifs with tape to form several repeats, and cut a stencil from a large sheet of acetate. This will take some time to prepare, but will be invaluable over a large surface area.

■ You can use a lightly loaded foam roller (usually used to apply gloss paint) instead of a fitch brush when stenciling. Always make sure the roller is completely dry before you begin. Any moisture will dilute the paint, causing it to run under the stencil. As with brush stenciling, do not overload the roller; work out the excess paint on the flat of the roller tray.

■ If used on a small feature wall area, this technique will not use much paint, so you may find it more economical to use tubes of acrylic or stencil paints, these come in a range of colors.

The sunny shades of yellow brighten up any room, and this easy colorwash technique is a great way to enliven any room, but particularly an informal, often-used room.

multi-toned colorwash

When two colorwashes are worked one over the other, a third color is created, and the broken color effect means that three tones mingle together on the same wall.

The first coat of burnt orange adds warmth and depth to the overall effect and looks quite strong when washed straight over a white base coat. This color is then considerably "knocked back" with the second coat of yellow ocher, but overall the warm hue is retained. Due to the fact that the colors are muting each other, the execution of the technique is not dramatically important, though patches should not be overpainted as this will start to lift the color off. Quick, broad brush strokes create a good, open effect.

Layering a lighter color over a darker one, as here, greatly softens the strength of the first shade and its brush marks. To layer a darker shade over a lighter one creates a stronger overall effect. The two colors need to have a similar tonal value for this effect to work: the palest of yellow base coats would not stand up to a strong orange.

Groundwork This effect will both disguise and emphasize any defects in the wall, resulting in an overall uneven effect. As the technique involves wiping a wash over the wall, any dents or cracks will be picked out with the brush strokes. But as the strokes are at random angles, the whole surface will look uneven. The extremes will then be flattened out with the application of the second layer, as the lighter color serves to mute the final effect. You can therefore choose to fill an uneven surface, or leave its flaws. Prepare the surface according to your choice, following the instructions on pages 18–19.

1 The first colorwash Mix 2 parts wallpaper paste with 1 part burnt orange matte latex paint in a paint pail and stir thoroughly. Dip the tips of a 4" (100mm) paintbrush into the mixture and scrape off the excess on the rim of the pail. Starting in a top corner, apply dabs of the wash to an area of a manageable size, such as a rough square of about 36" (900mm).

MATERIALS AND TOOLS	
■ Burnt orange matte latex paint	■ Wallpaper paste
■ Yellow ocher matte latex paint	■ 4" (100mm) paintbrush
	■ Paint pail

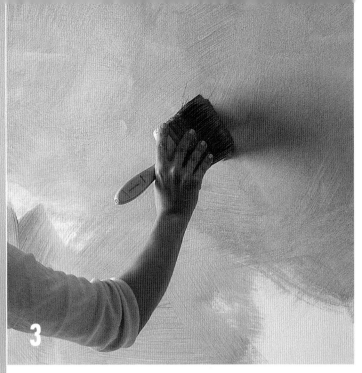

2 Brushing out While the wash is still wet and without adding any more wash to the brush, immediately brush these dabs out in random directions in large sweeping strokes, to join the wash marks together and create a light, translucent colorwash.

3 Moving on Move on to an adjacent area of about the same size. Apply the wash in random dabs and brush it out using sweeping brush strokes, as in Steps 1 and 2. Blend the edge of this second patch in with the edge of the first area using the dry brush.

4 Keep colorwashing Continue applying the colorwash by working in manageable areas and blending the patches together with a dry brush. Hold the brush by the bristles and flick it outward in random directions, to keep the look textured, natural, and not regimented. Keep the random look and work the edges. Do not apply dabs of wash right up to the edge of the wall. Instead use the dry brush on its side to blend the wash up to the corners. Leave to dry thoroughly.

5

The second colorwash

Mix 2 parts wallpaper paste with 1 part yellow ocher matte latex paint in a clean paint pail and stir thoroughly. Dip the tips of a clean 4" (100mm) paintbrush into the mixture and apply dabs of the second wash over the previous wash. Work in areas of a manageable size, but don't follow the pattern of patches used for the first colorwash coat.

Colorwashing again

Without adding any more wash to the brush, use it in sweeping strokes to join the paint patches and create a light allover finish. Continue by following Steps 2–4 until the whole wall area is covered. Once dry, any patches that are too thin can be lightly brushed over again with a minimal amount of wash, to even out the effect.

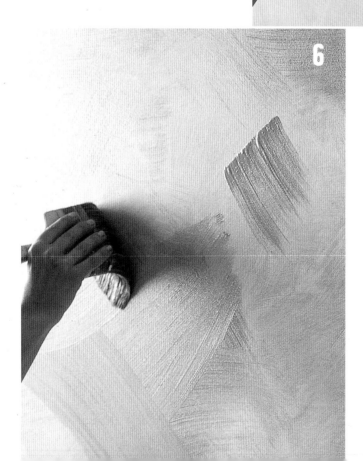

Trade secrets

■ Any washed effect relies on the broken color work for its look, but should also appear neat. To sharpen up the finish another wash layer can be added around the edges to make the paint appear more solid in these parts. Also paint the baseboard and cornice a solid color.

The ancient art of mosaic is timeless. However, the real thing is both time consuming and expensive, whereas a mosaic paint effect is attractive and can be changed as often as you wish.

stamped mosaic

This approach to creating a painted mosaic tile effect uses a stamp cut from high-density foam rubber and three paint colors used separately and partially blended. Since the overall effect is visually strong, it is a good idea to limit the pattern to a small area, rather than covering a whole wall, which could be overpowering. The area between a dado rail and the baseboard is the perfect place to apply this finish.

Groundwork The upper part of the wall must be completely smooth since it is painted in a flat solid color that will show all defects, so the usual procedure of filling, sanding, and priming must be followed. The actual mosaic stamp will disguise and cover almost any flaw as the paint is so thick and the pattern and color so varied. Any holes that aren't filled on the first stamp can be touched in with an artist's brush. Prepare the surface accordingly, following the instructions on pages 18–19.

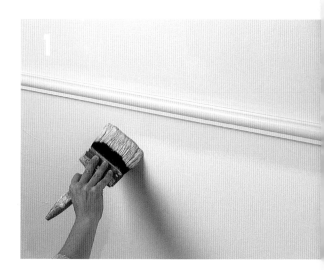

1 The base coat Apply two coats of pale beige matte latex paint to the whole wall area (including over the dado rail) using a roller or large paintbrush. Use a 1" (25mm) paintbrush to cut in at the edges. Leave the first coat to dry before applying the second, and allow the second coat to dry before moving on to the next step.

MATERIALS AND TOOLS				
	■ Pale beige matte latex paint	■ Roller and roller tray	■ Small artist's brush	■ Ruler
	■ Orange matte latex paint	■ Large paintbrush	■ Low-tack masking tape	■ Repositionable spray glue
	■ Red matte latex paint	■ Three 1" (25mm) brushes	■ Paper	■ High-density foam rubber
			■ Pencil	■ Craft knife

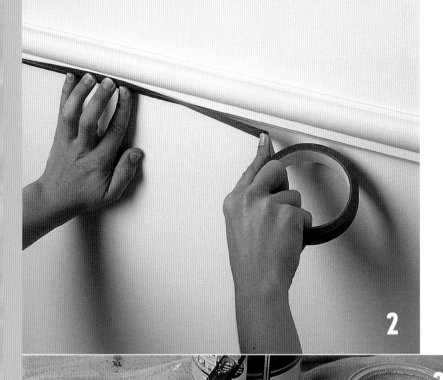

2 Masking Use low-tack masking tape to mask off the underside of the dado rail and along the top of the baseboard to isolate the area to be painted.

3 Preparing the paint Pour a little of each of the three paint colors, beige, orange, and red, into the well of a clean roller tray, one on each side and one in the middle. Matte latex paints are usually thick enough not to run straight into each other.

4 Partial blending Use a different, clean brush for each color and dab generous amounts onto the flat surface of the roller tray. Blend the colors a little in places, but do not mix the colors thoroughly as you still want a number of different colors to be apparent.

5

Making the stamp To make the stamp, cut some high-density foam rubber using a sharp craft knife. Make a paper template of 1" (25mm) squares butted closely together with rounded corners. Fix the template to the foam using repositionable spray glue. Cut around each line with the craft knife and remove the cutout parts of the template as you go. Carefully pinch out the remaining channels. The larger the stamp is cut the quicker and easier the stamping will be. Press the stamp into the paint until it is well coated, but not dripping with excess paint.

6

Stamping Starting in the top left-hand corner of the wall area under the dado rail, position the stamp on the surface and press down, taking care not to let the stamp slip.

7

Completing the stamping Pull the stamp cleanly away from the surface, peeling it back from one side. The overall printed look should be mottled without the different colors blending together too much and becoming muddy. Recoat the stamp, adding more paint to the palette when necessary, and continue stamping the wall by positioning the stamp next to the previous print, leaving a small gap in between to imitate the grout line. When you come to stamp the rows below the first row, remember that the vertical tiles should line up. Continue until completed and leave to dry.

6

Trade secrets

- If any of the painted mosaic tiles have bled onto the next, use a small artist's brush to paint in a line of the base color to separate them.

7

Golden Hues

The lively tones of yellows and oranges can be used to create finishes suitable for all rooms from bathrooms to bedrooms, and can be used in all techniques from stippling to stenciling—it is the ultimate versatile palette.

◀ Subtle sponging

Lemon yellow forms a good base coat for a pale green sponging effect (see pages 102–105), as the two tones are subtle enough to sit together pleasantly; the overall result is a fresh and clean feel to this bathroom.

▶ Sponged wash

A quick and easy paint effect to cover large areas such as stairs and landings is a colorwash (see pages 20–21). And, if you want to soften the look, you can avoid paintbrush marks by using the sponging technique (see pages 102–105).

◀ Aged paint

Candle wax and petroleum jelly are used as barriers between layers of paint to produce this antique effect. Select differing tones of yellow matte latex paint, and paint a solid coat of the darkest shade. When dry, apply long brush strokes of petroleum jelly to the surface, keeping it randomly spaced to imitate a wood grain. The jelly will not dry out, so it can be painted over immediately. Gently lay on the second darkest shade of yellow, without smearing the jelly too much. When this coat is dry, scrape it and the jelly away using a paint scraper, then wash the surface down with soapy water to make sure all the jelly has been removed. Now rub candle wax onto the surface in the same direction as the scraped paint, then solidly paint with the lightest yellow. When dry, scrape back the paint over the areas of wax. The petroleum jelly creates larger distressed patches than the candle wax, so using the two together provides an effective layering technique.

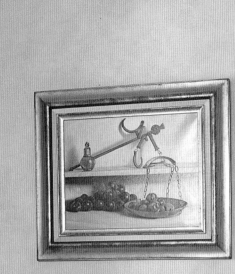

◄ **Basket weave**

This is a structured, tighter version of colorwashing using only a 1″ (25mm) paintbrush. To keep a "wicker" feel to the effect a yellow ocher is used over a flat white base coat. Mix together equal amounts of yellow ocher matte latex paint and water or wallpaper paste. Brush the wash on in long sections then create the basket weave pattern by marking "V" shapes in rows into the wet mixture with the 1″ (25mm) paintbrush. Continue with the next section, slightly overlapping the last.

◄ Roller fidget

This is one of the quickest and simplest of all paint techniques, and is, therefore, suited to large wall areas. In its simplest form it is a quick way of partially blending two colors directly on the wall. The choice of tones is important, since the colors must not make a muddy third color when mixed. Here a clean pale yellow and orange have been used together because they blend well and are similarly toned, so neither one is more dominant than the other. To add an extra dimension to the finish, a different colored base coat, white, which is not completely covered, is used, to keep the roller fidget effect light. Pour the two shades of matte latex paint into the same tray and gently swirl them around so that they are lightly mixed but not completely blended. Apply the paint to the wall with the roller as usual. You can also blend the colors while wet on the wall by angling the roller on each stroke. Using a long-haired masonry roller will also provide an interesting print.

► Clay wall

Colorwashing is a useful technique for imitating the chalky feel of unfinished clay. Since this effect attempts to recreate a particular surface, the color variations are limited to clay base colors with a pale cream for the chalky top layer. Brush a thick, undiluted layer of a clay-colored matte latex paint over white in random directions, achieving a semi-solid mottled effect when dry. Mix together 1 part pale cream matte latex paint and 3 parts water or wallpaper paste and colorwash the base (see Steps 1–4, pages 44–47); two layers of the cream wash may be needed to imitate a very powdery texture.

◄ Subtle stippling

This technique involves making pinpoint marks in a wash by dabbing the surface with a stippling brush: a large flat-fronted block of bristles. Over a clean orange base coat, apply a pure white wash, mixed with equal amounts of matte latex paint and water or wallpaper paste. Dab the bristles of the stippling brush into the wet wash to create an array of tiny dots. The overall effect is quite subtle, so if you prefer a stronger look, use contrasting tones.

► Stenciled border

Creating a decorative border is a quick way of reviving an existing scheme, and using a border stencil is a great way to create a strong look with only minimal effort. Borders are usually horizontal bands around a room at dado rail, picture rail, or ceiling height, but can also create frames as a feature or as vertical bands. Use an acetate border stencil that is easy to match up when producing the repeat pattern (see Steps 1–5, pages 40–42). Dry brush (see Step 4, page 68) the stencil with a very thin wash mixed from 1 part pale cream matte latex paint and 3 parts water or wallpaper paste, to give a dusty feel to the painting.

◄ Modern pattern

Colorwashing can make an effective base for other patterns or borders. Mix together equal amounts of muted yellow matte latex paint and water or wallpaper paste, and use a large brush to randomly apply a colorwash (see Steps 1–4, pages 44–47). To offset the cloudy background, draw strong geometric circles onto the wall and solidly paint them in using undiluted muted yellow paint. An alternative to hand painting the circles would be to cut a stamp from foam or use an acetate stencil (see Steps 1–5, pages 40–42 and Steps 5–7, pages 49–50).

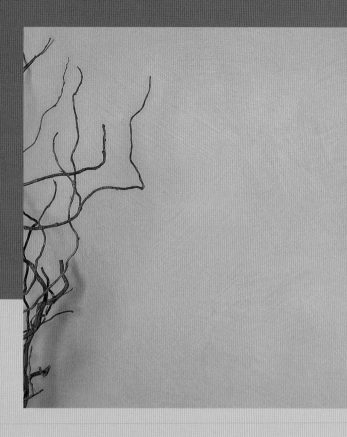

red · terra-cotta · claret

One of the key elements when designing interiors that you'll love to live with is creating an atmosphere. If you look at the influences of the tropics, where the sun beats down day after day, you'll find that the colors that generate a sense of well-being are rich reds and earthy terra-cottas. Walking into a room decorated with the varied shades and tones of this palette can be an uplifting experience: they envelop the room, creating a positive, welcoming atmosphere in a way that cooler colors of the spectrum cannot.

These colors are particularly rich, so they generally sit well with other sumptuous tones acting as contrasts, such as navy blue or jade green, while flat colors, such as taupe, can act to temper the overall effect.

Though this palette encompasses some of the warmest tones of the color wheel—scarlet, burgundy, eggplant—they can appear very heavy and dark, so should be used either as broken color work or in limited areas.

Recreate the softness of cotton and the pattern of a favorite fabric on your walls with the simple dry brushing technique, and bring a touch of relaxed elegance to your room.

sophisticated stripes

This finish attempts to imitate the soft look of stripes on fabric. None of the colors are painted solidly or with hard edges, while the tones are kept quite strong because they are contained in small areas. The technique hinges on dry brushing to create the fabric-like texture, and each color is roughly layered over the base coat. When planning this effect look at real striped fabric for successful color combinations.

The base color chosen here is a neutral tone, which sits well under all the different colors chosen for the stripes.

The overall visual impact is more decorative than most paint effects, so very little extra decoration will be required in the room.

The time element should be carefully considered before embarking on this design. Don't start by making thin lines close together, as finishing such a task will become laborious; remember that more stripes can always be added in at a later date.

Groundwork This effect has quite a rough finish so can tolerate a certain level of unevenness in the state of the wall. Though it would still be recommended that all obvious dents and cracks be filled and primed before painting, it is not necessary to go to the extent of lining or plastering the walls. Prepare the surface accordingly, following the instructions on pages 18–19.

1 The base coat Pour some beige matte latex paint into a paint pail. This coat needs to be kept light, so make sure that only a little paint is added to the brush each time. Dip the tips of a 4″ (100mm) paintbrush into the paint and scrape off the excess on the rim of the pail. Holding the bristles of the brush almost parallel to the wall, apply the paint in a vertical direction using just the tip of the brush to release only a little paint, for a loose effect.

MATERIALS AND TOOLS

- Beige matte latex paint
- Dark red matte latex paint
- Orange matte latex paint
- Dark blue matte latex paint
- 4″ (100mm) paintbrush
- Two 2″ (50mm) paintbrushes
- Lining brush
- Paint pail
- Pencil
- Tape measure
- Ruler
- Carpenter's level

2 Brushing out Without adding more paint to the brush, keep working the brush into the paint so that you obtain a fairly solid covering, but with a little of the white undercoat showing through in places. The finished effect should be lightly textured, not flat color. Continue in the same way to cover the whole wall. Leave to dry.

2

3

4

3 Planning the stripes Plan the size and spacing you are going to use for the three bands of different colors. The scheme illustrated uses 12" (300mm) bands of orange, 5" (130mm) bands of dark red, and a single freehand painted line of dark blue. Use a pencil, tape measure, and ruler to lightly draw in all the vertical lines. Use a carpenter's level to make sure the lines are straight.

4 At the edge of a band Pour the orange matte latex paint into a clean paint pail and dip the tips of a 2" (50mm) paintbrush into the paint. Scrape off the excess paint along the rim of the pail and run the brush along the pencil line. This painted line should not be perfectly straight and sharp, but should look slightly broken. Repeat along the opposite pencil line that delineates the other edge of the orange band.

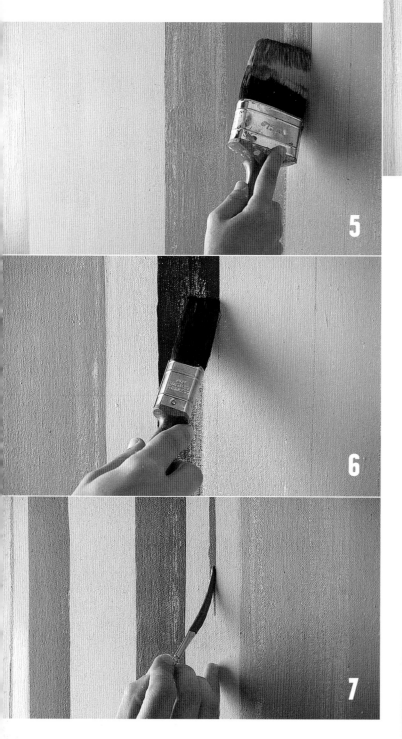

7 Fine lines To paint in a fine dark blue line, pour the paint into a clean paint pail and dip the tip of a lining brush into the paint. Scrape the excess off on the rim of the pail. Hold the brush against the pencil line and drag it down, applying only a little pressure. The effect should be quite broken. When the paint is dry, you can go over the thin line again if it is not pronounced enough. Complete all the blue lines in the same way.

8 Disguising mistakes Once the paint is dry, any mistakes can be touched up with the base color and a 2″ (50mm) paintbrush or a small artist's brush for truly intricate work.

Trade secrets

■ Dry brushing is a simple technique, which mainly relies on the amount of paint and pressure on the brush. A long-bristle brush will naturally apply less pressure to the wall than a short-bristle brush. Practice first by holding the brush almost parallel to the wall and then only applying more pressure on the stroke when there is less and less paint on the brush.

■ The overall effect of bands of color in a room can be very dramatic and overpowering so it can be a good idea to make up test sheets on paper to determine the best use of widths and colors.

■ Use quite a well loaded brush for all the straight edges to make painting the line easier.

5 Filling in Fill in the middle by using elongated dry brush strokes as described in Step 2, ensuring some of the beige base is still visible through the orange. Complete all the orange bands before moving on to the red stripes.

6 Working the next bands Fill in the narrower band with dark red by repeating Steps 4 and 5, using a clean paint pail and a clean, dry 2″ (50mm) paintbrush. Complete all the red bands before starting on the fine blue lines.

Colorwashing is the most simple of all paint effects, and is ideal for those who lead busy lives and have little time to spare, but it is also immensely powerful in reinventing the mood of a room.

one-on-one colorwash

This simple washed effect works with two layers of the same color. The standard of the technique is of little importance as the second layer serves to cover all mistakes. An overall mottled effect is created, the strength of which is determined by the thickness of the paint mixture. Using exact quantities is a good general rule. To make the effect more opaque add 2 parts paint to 1 part wallpaper paste and vice versa for a more mottled look.

Groundwork This effect will both disguise and emphasize any defects in the wall resulting in an overall uneven effect. As the technique involves wiping a wash over the wall any dents or cracks will be picked out with the brush strokes. But as the strokes themselves are at random angles the whole surface is made to look uneven. The second coat of wash will continue to make the whole wall appear uneven while flattening the overall effect. You can therefore choose to fill an uneven surface, or leave its flaws. Prepare the surface according to your choice, following the instructions on pages 18–19.

MATERIALS AND TOOLS

- Terra-cotta matte latex paint
- Wallpaper paste
- 4" (100mm) paintbrush
- Paint pail

1 **The first colorwash** Mix equal amounts of wallpaper paste and terra-cotta matte latex paint in a paint pail. Dip the tips of a 4" (100mm) paintbrush into the wash mixture and scrape off the excess on the rim of the pail. Starting in a top corner of the room, apply dabs of wash to the wall working on a manageable area of the wall, such as a rough square about 36" (900mm). While the wash is still wet and without adding any more wash to the brush, immediately brush these dabs out in random directions using large sweeping strokes to join the wash marks together and to create a light, translucent colorwash.

2 **Moving on** Move on to an adjacent area of about the same size. Apply the wash in random dabs and brush it out using sweeping brush strokes, as in Step 1. Blend the edge of this second patch in with the edge of the first area using the dry brush. Continue applying and blending the colorwash using random and sweeping brush strokes. Hold the brush by the bristles and flick it outward in random directions, to keep the look textured, natural, and not regimented. When you get to the edge of the room, run a line of the colorwash into the corner then blend it in with the rest of the paint effect using the dry brush.

3 **Keep colorwashing** Continue in the same way on the next wall, blending the patches of colorwash together and working into the corner with a dry brush. Leave to dry.

4 **The second colorwash** Use the same wash mixture to apply a second colorwash following Steps 1–3. Work in areas of a manageable size, but don't follow the pattern of patches used for the first coat. Try to work with a different pattern of areas. Remember to keep the brush strokes random. When the entire room is finished leave to dry thoroughly.

Trade secrets

- When painting into a corner, if the wash mixture gets onto the adjacent wall before you are ready to work it in with a dry brush, wipe it off immediately with a damp cloth.

- Any washed effect relies on the broken color work for its look, but should also appear neat. To sharpen up the finish, another wash layer can be added around the edges to make the paint appear more solid in these parts. Also paint the baseboard and cornice a solid color.

4

The dark tones of claret are ideal for rooms with real fires or book-filled studies—in the summer they reflect the warmth of outside, and in the winter they are cozy and welcoming.

two-tone dry brushing

The dry brushing technique uses undiluted paint, which is applied in random directions leaving a little base color exposed in places. This is a simple effect that layers one color over another to create texture and depth. As the paint is opaque, and no visual mixing occurs as with washes, any color combination can be tried, though a dark tone over a very light one will show streaks in the paint. The technique serves well in covering up uneven or pitted walls as it creates an overall unevenness made more effective on a poor surface. Speed is unimportant as the paint is undiluted and joins will not be as visible as with a wash, so the surface texture can be built up slowly.

Groundwork As dents and cracks in the wall enhance this effect it is a perfect technique for poor, old walls with only the minimal amount of preparation necessary. The walls should be washed down with a solution of TSP (trisodium phosphate) or sugar soap to remove any traces of dust or grease which would act as a barrier when the next coat of paint is applied, and primed. Prepare the surface accordingly, following the instructions on pages 18–19.

1 The base coat Pour red matte latex paint into a paint pail. Using a 4″ (100mm) paintbrush, apply the paint to the wall using large, random strokes. Continue across the wall until all the white is covered. The color will not be totally solid as one coat of dark red will not obliterate the white, but this does not matter since this coat is acting as a strong, mottled base tone that will also be mostly covered. Leave to dry thoroughly.

MATERIALS AND TOOLS

- Red matte latex paint
- Claret matte latex paint
- 4″ (100mm) paintbrush
- Paint pail

2

3

2 Loading the brush
The next coat needs to be kept light, so make sure that only a little paint is added each time, covering only the end of the bristles. Pour claret matte latex paint into a clean paint pail. Dip the tips of a clean 4″ (100mm) brush into the paint and scrape off the excess on the rim of the pail.

3 Dry brushing Hold the brush almost parallel to the surface, and apply the paint using just the tip of the brush to release only a little paint for a loose effect. Turn the brush over to use the paint on the other side of the bristles and change the angle of the strokes for a random effect. As there is less and less paint left on the brush you can begin to brush more vigorously.

4

5

4 **Continuing the effect** Continue across the whole wall in the same way, only adding more paint to the tips of the bristles when the brush stops releasing color completely. Ensure a reasonable amount of the first color remains visible.

5 **Finishing** Stand back from the wall to judge the evenness of the effect and add more paint where necessary. Keep the areas up to the baseboard and ceiling quite solid as this will make the effect look neater.

Trade secrets

■ The effect can be made to appear "tighter" by using shorter brush strokes while a "looser" look requires longer, more sweeping brush strokes.

▶ Dramatic damask

A damask is a self-patterned fabric. The pattern is either made up of a gloss finish on a matte surface, or a heavy, solid version of the less dense background fabric. The latter idea was used in this effect. Create a soft, two layer colorwash in red over white as the base (see pages 62–65). Use the undiluted paint to stencil a repeat pattern on top (see pages 40–43). If the finished effect is too harsh, colorwash the surface again, over the stenciling, to soften the effect.

◀ Soft stenciling

A delicate feathery stencil can bring a touch of sophistication to a room, by appearing just on occasional panels (see pages 80–83). Here a pinkish-white has been painted over a light terra-cotta wash to create a soft yet stylish overall effect.

Red-Hot Rooms

Bring a touch of spice to your walls by introducing the ambient tones of pink, scarlet, and burgundy. Whether you choose to opt for a demure damask print, a striking check, or an opulent crackle glaze, the red palette will never fail to make an impression on a room.

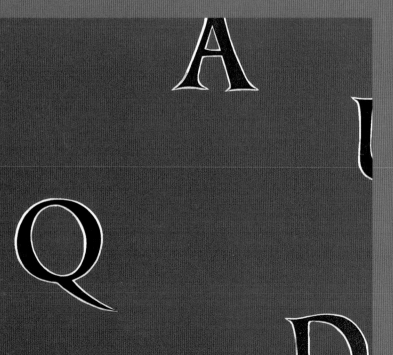

◀ Découpage

The découpage technique is a simple way to decorate existing room schemes without any painting. Research motifs, initials, patterns, or pictures—here formal lettering was chosen—and photocopy them, enlarging or reducing if required. The only work is in the cutting; the more accurate the trimming the better the look. Use a metal ruler, craft knife, and sharp cuticle scissors to cut neatly around all the edges. The motifs are then arranged over a solid painted wall—a smart, deep red provides the background in this case. The positioning of the motifs can be completely random, or organized using careful measurements and light pencil marks. To fix the photocopies to the wall, apply wallpaper paste to the back of them. Leave the paste for a few minutes to soak in. Position the motif on the wall and brush it flat with a clean, dry brush.

▲ Kitchen inspiration

If you feel that your options for reinventing a room are limited by the room's existing elements, take another look at those elements to see if there is anything you can take from them. For example, this simple stencil's pattern has beein inspired by the flower motif on the drapes, whereas the color was taken from the crockery.

▶ Paper frottage

This technique imitates the surface of the
tool used to create it. Over a deep red
base coat, randomly brush on a wash mixed
from equal amounts of pale terra-cotta
matte latex paint and water or wallpaper
paste. Lay some slightly scrunched up
newspaper over the top of the wet wash; as
this is quite porous much of the wash will
soak in and many sheets will be needed.
When the newspaper is lifted the print left
in the wash mimics the folds in the paper.
The effect should be achieved in one print,
but if it is poor, brush the wash over again
before trying a second print. The effect
here is subtle because a lighter color is used
over a darker one—the look would be
more dramatic if the colors were used in
the reverse order.

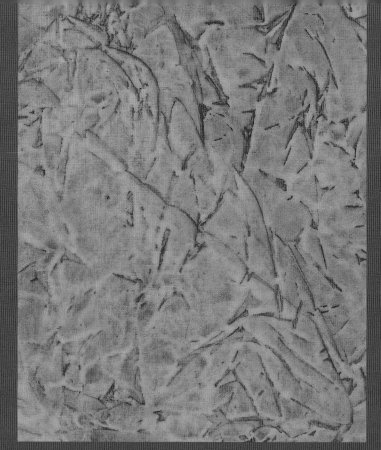

◀ Marbling

Marbling is one of the most
traditional and difficult paint
effects. For a professional finish,
artist's oil colors, specialty
brushes, and a lot of practice
are required if any sense of
realism is to be achieved.
Illustrated here is a simpler
method. Mix washes using
equal amounts of natural earthy
sienna tones of matte latex
paint and water or wallpaper
paste. Use two of the
techniques described above
and opposite, paper frottage
and chenille effect, in any
order, to build up layers,
making sure each layer is dry
before the next is applied.
When you are happy with the
effect, use a lining brush to
paint in gray veins. Try to
match the colors from real
marble, as this will greatly
improve the overall result.

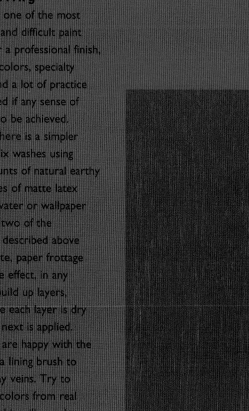

◄ Sharp squares

A simple approach to creating sharp squares with equal spacing is to paint a grid of horizontal and vertical bands. The size and proportion of the squares should be planned carefully, considering the effect can be visually intense. The stripes are applied with a 4″ (100mm) paint pad. Over a beige base coat, draw guidelines onto the wall using a carpenter's level. Only one line is needed for each stripe since the paint pad used determines the width, only if the band is to be wider than the widest paint pad should two lines be needed. Use the paint pad to apply bands of eggplant matte latex paint.

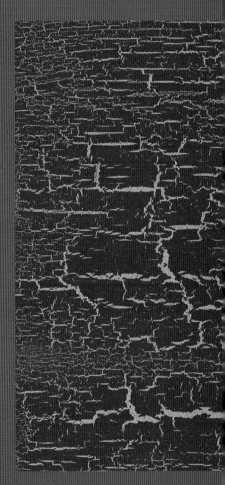

► Crackle glaze

The crackle glaze medium causes a top paint coat to crack, revealing the base color. The general look mimics old cracked paint, but is usually more exaggerated and even than the real thing. For a traditional look, use a paintbrush to apply the specialty crackle glaze over a solid gold matte latex paint base coat. When dry, paint over the glaze with deep claret red matte latex paint, using brush strokes in one direction only. Then sit back and watch the top coat crack as it dries. Usually the cracks are larger when a thick coat of glaze is applied, but each product varies so read the instructions carefully for guidance. Any combinations of colors can be used: the more extreme the stronger the effect.

◄ Chenille effect

Chenille is a rich fabric containing two differing tones of the same color. To imitate the depth of chenille, two tones of red are used, a primary red solid base coat and a deep claret colorwash (see Steps 1–4, pages 44–45), keeping the brushmarks in the wash quite obvious. The look of woollen strands can be made using lengths of plastic food wrap pulled tightly at each end and laid on the wet wash to create ribs. For a softer effect, use the primary red as the wash over the darker, solid base color.

blue · navy · violet

This palette is based on the variations of blue, mixed with grays to create navy, or mixed with reds to produce violet tones. With such a broad range, the opportunity to produce a breadth of different atmospheres in the home is at your fingertips.

Rich navy blues suit a smart, classic interior, so in a formal room, such as a dining area used for entertaining, there is no better way to set a traditional mood than to add strict touches of navy. Using violet or mauve, on the other hand, has a softer effect, but can still look smart when used in a regimented way.

The blue to violet palette runs through great tonal extremes, from pale blue and lilac to navy and violet, so overall effects can be starkly different. It is wise to consider the colors as pale, bright, and dark individually, and mix and match other colors within those perimeters, though the best schemes are often achieved using the blue and violet tones together. If another color is to be added, use it as an accent color in a limited area, such as orange stripes through navy blue.

Bring the seaside into your home with this nautical look. The colors used here particularly suit the waterworld of a bathroom, and are sure to freshen up the dullest of rooms.

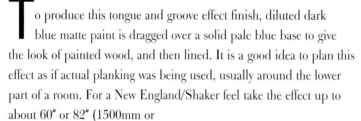

tongue and groove tricks

To produce this tongue and groove effect finish, diluted dark blue matte paint is dragged over a solid pale blue base to give the look of painted wood, and then lined. It is a good idea to plan this effect as if actual planking was being used, usually around the lower part of a room. For a New England/Shaker feel take the effect up to about 60″ or 82″ (1500mm or 2000mm) high and top with a shelf or peg rail to neatly finish off the look.

Groundwork The wall must be in very good condition for this finish, not only for the solid painted section but also for the paint effect below. Dragging and lining techniques both need to be carried out on a flat, smooth surface. Any obvious dents or cracks will ruin the lines, which need to be as straight as possible for the effect to work. Therefore, any old plaster should be lined and primed before this technique is tried. Prepare the surface accordingly, following the instructions on pages 18–19.

1 The base coat Paint two solid coats of pale blue over the whole wall and leave to dry.

MATERIALS AND TOOLS	■ Pale blue matte latex paint ■ Dark blue matte latex paint ■ 2″ (50mm) paintbrush	■ Dragging brush ■ Lining brush ■ Paint pail ■ Low-tack masking tape ■ Tape measure ■ Pencil	■ Ruler ■ Carpenter's level

2 **Marking the height of the panels** Use a tape measure and pencil to mark off lightly points across the wall at a height of anywhere between 60″ or 82″ (1500mm or 2000mm). Use a ruler to join the marks and draw a level line across the wall. Use a carpenter's level to check the line is completely straight before continuing.

3 **Masking** Run strips of masking tape all along the wall on top of the pencil lines.

4 **Applying diluted paint** Mix equal amounts of dark blue matte latex paint and water in a paint pail. Dip a clean paintbrush into the diluted paint and scrape off the excess on the rim of the pail. Working in manageably sized strips, brush the paint vertically onto the wall, starting from one corner.

5 **Dragging** Hold a dragging brush in one hand and place your other hand near the tip of the bristles—this will help you control the brush. Pull the brush down through the wet paint, trying to keep the line as straight as possible. Run over the paint again while it is still wet if the drag isn't straight enough. Brush on the next section of paint, slightly overlapping the previous strip, and drag as before. Leave to dry.

6 Marking the planks

Draw vertical pencil lines over the paint effect at 6″ (150mm) intervals all across the wall. These lines will imitate the shadows that differentiate the "planks" of the faux tongue and groove.

7 Painting in the planks Using a lining brush and the diluted dark blue paint, go over the pencil lines. When lining long verticals such as these, hold the lining brush downward and start at the bottom, working up. This will make the long bristles and possible drips easier to control. When reapplying the brush to the line after reloading, start by slightly overlapping the previously painted line, helping to create a straighter, more consistent line. Use an even pressure and a steady hand to create uniform straight lines. Leave to dry, then remove the masking tape to finish.

Trade secrets

■ It can be helpful to hang a plumbline at intervals while you drag; this will work as a guide and will help to keep the effect straight.

This delicate look befits a romantic bedroom. While care must be taken to ensure the stencil is applied cleanly and crisply, it is, nevertheless, an easy technique to pick up.

feathery finishes

For this unique effect, white paint is stenciled over pale mauve using a custom-made feather stencil. The technique used is a simple approach creating an allover wallpaper pattern, but without the extra work of measuring, marking, or matching up any patterns. The same motif is used at constantly alternating angles based on the appearance of a falling feather.

When choosing a motif to be used randomly, look at shapes that would make sense as a pattern on wallpaper and that can appear at different angles. Natural objects always provide a wealth of material as long as they have an easily identifiable outline shape.

To make the stencil, draw or trace your chosen design onto a piece of clean, white paper. Tape the paper to a cutting mat, then tape a sheet of acetate over the paper. Use a craft knife to cut the acetate to the design. Acetate will create a more durable stencil than card.

Groundwork This is one effect where the surface of the wall must be perfect. If the stencil is painted over any uneven surface the pattern will distort the surface or bleed under the stencil. Therefore, only apply this effect to new plaster or heavy duty lining paper. Prepare the surface accordingly, following the instructions on pages 18–19.

MATERIALS AND TOOLS

- Pale mauve matte latex paint
- White matte latex paint
- 4" (100mm) paintbrush
- Paint pail
- Large fitch brush
- Feather stencil
- Low-tack masking tape
- Roller tray

1 **The base coat** Dip the tips of a 4″ (100mm) paintbrush into a pail of pale mauve matte latex paint. Scrape off the excess paint on the rim of the paint pail. Starting in a top corner of the room, apply dabs of paint to the wall working in a manageable area of the wall, such as a rough square about 36″ (900mm). While the paint is still wet, and without adding any more paint to the brush, immediately brush these dabs out in random directions, using large sweeping strokes, to join the paint marks together and create a lightly textured painted background. Continue working in patches across the wall, using the dry brush to blend the areas together, until the surface is completely covered. Leave to dry thoroughly.

1

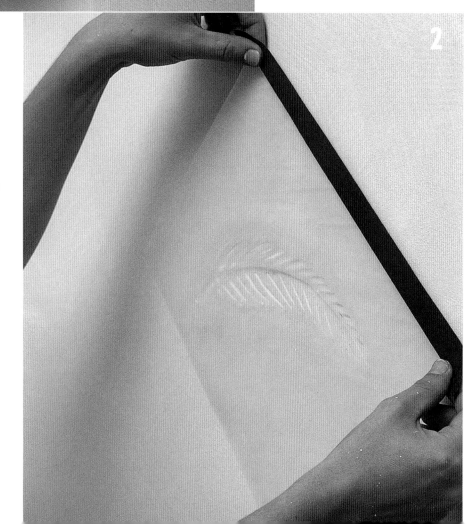

2

2 **Preparing the stencil** Tear off a length of low-tack masking tape about the size of the stencil width. Press the tape against your clothing to remove excess tack and lessen the chance of it removing any paint from the wall. Press the tape along the top of the stencil, this allows you to lift and check the print while painting without having to painstakingly reposition and realign the stencil by hand. Press the stencil onto the wall in the first, random position.

3 Stenciling Pour a little white matte latex paint into the well of a clean roller tray, keeping the paint contained and providing an area on the flat section for dabbing off excess paint. Dip the tips of a large fitch brush into the paint and dab off the excess. When stenciling always use the paint sparingly. Stencil over the pattern by dabbing the flat of the brush over the surface in a pouncing motion. Add more paint when needed, but sparingly. If at any point a motif seems to be awkwardly placed, allow it to dry then simply paint over it using the base color, then reposition and stencil again.

4 To continue Lift the stencil while it is still fixed to the wall by the line of tape, and check that it is evenly covered with paint. If necessary, replace the stencil and go over unpainted areas again. Peel the stencil back and carefully roll the tape away from the wall. Reposition the stencil, changing its angle. Never place the stencil directly below, above, or to either side of another print. Apply the white paint as in Step 3. Continue stenciling all across the wall, randomly positioning the stencil and changing its angle. Keep standing back to view your work, until the wall appears to be full.

Trade secrets

■ With delicate stencils the paint must be applied very gently so that it does not bleed under any of the narrow bridges—the small strips that join the design. Always ensure that the stencil is clean and that the brush is completely dry before use: a moist brush will dilute the paint, making it more likely to bleed.

The polished, yet textured, look of this richly colored project may take some time to achieve, but the result is well worth it. Don't be afraid to use the oil colors, they are as simple to apply as paint.

polished plaster

This paint effect imitates the look of smooth polished plaster—a glossy finish that is not usually associated with fresh plaster, particularly when it is bright blue.

The finish should always be worked using two tones of the same color. Using a lighter tone over a darker one will create a chalky effect, characteristic of unfinished plaster, while a darker shade over a lighter tint will produce a finished, polished look. For a dramatic effect use strong, bold tones, like the two bright blues used here. To add extra depth, finish with a layer of oil-based varnish for a rich, glossy appearance. When choosing a lighter allover scheme, always use the lighter tone over the darker one, otherwise the effect will be hard to see.

Because this project uses artist's oil color, the completed surface will take at least two days to dry. If it is then sealed with an oil-based varnish, the walls will need to be sanded back before they can be repainted at a later date. However, oil-based products are slow drying, which gives you plenty of time to manipulate the glaze and achieve a perfect finish.

Groundwork The walls must be totally smooth for this paint effect to work. New plaster is a perfect finish as long as it is treated with plaster seal beforehand to make the surface less porous. Prepare the surface accordingly, following the instructions on pages 18–19.

1 The base coat Pour the mid-blue matte latex paint into a paint pail. Dip the tips of a 4″ (100mm) paintbrush into the paint and scrape off the excess on the rim of the pail. Starting in a top corner of the room, apply dabs of color to the surface, working in an area of the wall that is of a manageable size, such as a rough square about 36″ (900mm).

MATERIALS AND TOOLS

- Mid-blue matte latex paint
- White artist's oil color
- Ultramarine blue artist's oil color
- Boiled linseed oil
- Mineral spirits
- 4″ (100mm) paintbrush
- Paint pail
- Grout float

2 **Brushing out** While the paint is still wet, and without adding any more paint to the brush, immediately brush these dabs out in random directions using large sweeping strokes, to join the paint marks together and create a lightly textured background. Continue working in patches across the wall, using the dry brush to blend adjacent areas. Leave to dry.

3 **The oil glaze** Mix ultramarine blue and white artist's oil colors with equal quantities of mineral spirits and boiled linseed oil in a clean paint pail, until the mixture is a paler blue than the base color and has the consistency of thin cream. Load a clean 4" (100mm) paintbrush with this oil glaze and brush it onto the surface, spreading it out as far as possible.

4 **Smoothing out** Immediately take a clean grout float and hold it flat to the surface. Work the float over the wet glaze, smearing out all the visible brush marks. Using a grout float is a similar technique to plastering a wall, however, a smooth finish is not necessary, rather make small angled strokes in the wet glaze to create a textured plaster finish.

5 Sharp finishing
Finish the grout float strokes by stopping at sharp alternating diagonals where the paint collects and leaves strong marks.

Trade secrets

■ When mixing the oil glaze, keep a reference of the quantities of each color, mineral spirits, and boiled linseed oil used. Reproducing the exact color is difficult so this will act as a recipe.

■ The boiled linseed oil in the mix acts to thicken the glaze, and is also the element that takes so long to dry. Try and balance it out with as much mineral spirits as possible but not so much that the mixture becomes too runny.

■ Even when the wall is touch dry, the paint may still lift when applying a varnish, so test out a small area that won't be seen before you work on the whole wall. If the paint does lift off, leave it for at least another day before testing again.

◄ Trompe l'oeil mural

Add a touch of drama to your home by painting a trompe l'oeil on an end wall (see pages 112–115). This impressive "plaster mural" jumps out of the wall at you, and a second look is needed to realize that it is actually a flat painting.

Moody Blues

Shades of sky and sea are incredibly atmospheric, and depending on what effect you use, whether it be a fresh blue checked border, a brooding skyscape, or clean, sharp stripes, you can create any feel from bright to moody to formal.

▲ Cloudy sky

Classic soft fluffy clouds, painted as horizontal, long narrow shapes across a flat, clean blue base coat, traditionally appear only on ceilings, but there is no reason why this can't be applied to a wall. Two solid coats of pale, clean blue form the base coat. Create the clouds by diluting 3 parts white matte latex paint with 1 part wallpaper paste. Use a fitch brush to stipple the wash onto the wall in a pouncing motion, starting at the top cloud shape line then blending downward as the paint runs out. When more paint is added to the brush repeat the process. To add a sense of realism, the size of the cloud should decrease toward the bottom of the wall, imitating a horizon line. More sophisticated versions can play on grading the base color (see pages 98–101) or adding sunset tones blended together; adjust the cloud colors accordingly, taking inspiration from photographs or pictures.

◄ Hazy shades

A soft colorwash is applied with a sponge to create a mottled, almost fluffy final appearance. The white base coat is overpainted with a wash mixed from equal amounts of lilac matte latex paint and water or wallpaper paste. Rub the wash onto the wall with the sponge using circular motions, then "lay off" any obvious smears before the wash dries by lightly buffing the surface (see Step 1, page 30). The whole process can be repeated for a softer appearance, using a similarly toned second wash. Using two tones of the same color avoids any muddy effects created by a bad combination; test out any combination beforehand.

► Cricket stripes

Clean narrow stripes in regimented rows are generally known as cricket stripes. This formal effect was made subtler here by using a solid lupin blue over a solid white base coat, then enhanced with thin navy blue lines. Thin stripes can be time consuming to produce, but using a narrow 1" (25mm) paint pad is the quickest way to achieve straight-edged stripes of a constant width. Draw vertical pencil guidelines with a carpenter's level to ensure an accurate finish. Experiment with the spacing of the stripes but be careful not to make the look too visually confusing, as the effect is strong.

▲ Country colorwash

This comfortable rustic room has been given a bold color scheme that adds immense character. The use of two colors—soft blue and violet—in colorwash also serves to create a sense of movement.

◄ Denim design

Recreating the look of denim with paint is achieved using the dragging technique (see Steps 4 and 5, page 78). Look at the tones of real denim when choosing paint colors, remembering how gray the fabric looks when washed out. Keep the blue-gray base coat quite flat and pale, with a darker blue-gray top coat wash mixed from roughly equal amounts of matte latex paint and wallpaper paste, to make a thick consistency that is weak in color. The thick consistency should hold the paint marks in place once the dragging brush is pulled through. A straight run is needed, so the technique is limited to sections of a wall no higher than standing height.

► Dry brush distress

To imitate the look of worn paint, without making it appear too old and flaking, just add another layer of paint similar to the last, but a little lighter. Here, three various tones of blue— dark blue, turquoise, and sky blue— are used, keeping the darker tone as the base color. Use a wide brush and the dry brushing technique (see pages 66–69) to apply long strokes of the second and third coats to the surface, always working from top to bottom and brushing out the paint as much as possible before adding any more. For further depth, several tones and layers can be used, but keep the brush strokes in the same direction and leaving a little of the previous colors exposed.

◄ Checked border

Using a decorative border is a quick and simple way to add interest to a plain wall. The checked effect here is emphasized by using a strong mid-blue over a flat, solid white base. Draw a horizontal line at chair or picture rail height, and cut a square from high-density foam rubber to use as a stamp for quick, exact shapes (see Step 5, page 49). Print from bottom to top, keeping the stamp straight and using the last square as a positioning guide (see Steps 6–7, pages 49–50). A bold checked band in a bright color is visually strong enough to effectively distract from a large expanse of flat color.

◄ Mottling

A mottled look uses the softest of colorwashes, showing the fewest application marks. Mix together equal amounts of pale mauve matte latex paint and water or wallpaper paste. Dip a large sponge into the wash and scrape off the excess wash. Apply the wash to the wall, over a white base coat, in a circular motion, then buff gently to remove any obvious smears (see Step 1, page 30). When the first colorwash is dry apply a second layer in the same way, aiming to produce a semi-solid effect at one end of the wall and gradually lightening the amount of wash applied, until you are left with only the first layer. This creates a sense of movement in the paint, taking the wall from a fairly bright mauve to a very pale lilac. For a dusty feel use a pale color over a darker shade, while the reverse (as here) creates a more solid look.

► Wash over metallic

A metallic sheen gives an unusual look, while random patterns of colorwash create a lively surface texture. Mix metallic paint with water to a medium consistency; brush on in sweeping movements. When dry, draw horizontal pencil lines about 12" (300mm) apart. Prepare three separate thin washes of the desired top colors, and apply the first color into a horizontal band, roughly painting the edges with a brush then filling in color to the center of the band with either a brush or a sponge with swirling movements to emphasize the metallic brush marks and to create interesting textures. While wet, add spots of other colors which will merge and blend into the main color. Repeat for each band.

turquoise · lime · dark green

Making a statement when decorating your home calls for the use of strong colors that have an instant impact. The turquoise palette, from blue-green to bright green, offers a diverse mix of shades and tones that can be used to add a bright splash of color to any room. Imagine how good it feels to sit under a bright blue sky with a sparkling green sea ahead of you, and bring this mood into your home.

Practically, it is a good idea to use greens and turquoise as accent colors, using them only on a feature wall, for example, and keeping the rest of the walls in a pale or neutral shade to add a fresh dash of color; used for whole rooms the colors from this palette can be very strong and may become overpowering, but will definitely appear bright and lively.

As with the blue to violet palette, the range of tones encompassed within turquoise is quite extreme, and in this case particularly bright, so coordinating tones within the same palette is more suitable than introducing outside hues.

This shimmering display takes advantage of the wide range of metallic paints now available. No specialist knowledge is needed to use these paints, and the results are quite exhilarating.

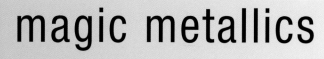

magic metallics

You can create a modern geometric wall-art effect quickly and easily by combining two simple paint techniques, colorwashing and stippling. This striking design is most effective when placed centrally on a wall, taking into account the fixtures, fittings, and furniture. For an original alternative, you can use the corner of your room as the central point of the design, allowing the shapes to extend onto two perpendicular walls. As usual, the key to a good finish is thorough preparation. Before you start to paint or even draw on the wall, plan out on paper the exact position, shape, and size of the desired image. Think carefully at this stage about the color combinations you intend to use.

Groundwork

As the design involves using flat color in localized areas, the surface of the wall to be painted must be smooth and in good condition, and any holes, dents, or cracks should be made good before you start. Fill blemishes with interior filler, leaving the surface slightly raised from the wall. When this has hardened, sand smooth with fine-grade sandpaper and wash the entire area with sugar soap. The wall is now ready to paint.

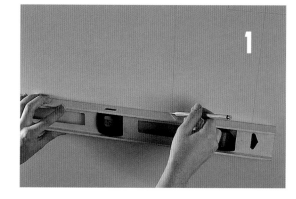

1 Base coat Apply a base coat of pale turquoise matte emulsion with a good quality roller, using a 1″ (25mm) or 2″ (50mm) household brush for the edges and corners. Two coats should give adequate coverage; allow each to dry for 4 to 6 hours. Using a carpenter's level, draw out the design on the wall with a pencil. Start by drawing the larger shapes, then add in the smaller overlapping sections on top. There are no strictly correct dimensions for the shapes; let your eye tell you what looks best.

MATERIALS AND TOOLS			
■ Pale turquoise matte emulsion ■ Silver acrylic wash ■ Pewter artist's acrylic ■ Solid silver gloss paint	■ Aquamarine gilt cream ■ 1″ (25mm) and 2″ (50mm) household brushes ■ Flat, square artist's brush	■ Soft-haired brush ■ Fitch brush ■ Paint roller and roller tray ■ Paint pail ■ Mineral spirits	■ Carpenter's level ■ Pencil ■ Low-tack masking tape ■ Scissors or craft knife

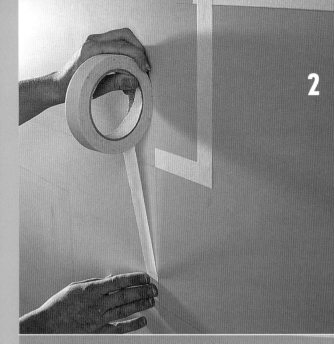

2

3

4

5

2 Masking off Paint over any unwanted pencil marks with an artist's brush, and once this has dried, mask off the outside of the largest area of color—in this case, the two pale silver blocks. Make sure that you do not cover the pencil guidelines, or you will discover when you remove the tape at the end that these are still visible. To keep the corners of the shapes sharp, cut the masking tape with scissors or a craft knife, rather than just tearing it.

3 Blank canvas Pour a little silver wash into a paint pail and carefully load the tip of a 2″ (50mm) brush. Apply the paint to the area bounded by the tape using small random strokes, ensuring the brush marks remain visible. Remove the tape carefully from the wet paint and leave to dry.

4 Second base Mask off the next section as described in Step 2. Squeeze half a tube of pewter artist's acrylic into a paint pail and add water until the mixture has the consistency of thin cream. Paint in the shape with small random strokes using the 2″ (50mm) brush.

5 Low-tack solution Remove the masking tape while the paint is still wet, taking great care that you don't accidentally take off any of the silver paint from the first shape as you pull the tape from the wall. Using low-tack masking tape makes this much less likely to occur. Leave to dry.

6 **Square three** Mask off the third shape, then apply the solid silver paint straight from the pot, using a soft-haired brush to minimize brush marks. Remove the tape and leave to dry.

7 **Home and dry** Mask off the remaining small overlapping shapes. Spoon half a pot of aquamarine gilt cream into a paint pail, blending with just a drop of mineral spirits to make the mixture slightly more liquid. Brush the paint onto the wall using a fitch brush then erase any brush strokes by stippling over the whole area with the same brush. Remove the tape and leave to dry. As the gilt cream is oil-based this may take some time—allow at least 4 hours. Finally, buff the finish to a shine with a soft cloth.

Trade secrets

■ Use a flat artist's brush loaded with pale turquoise to touch in mistakes or bleeding from the masking tape. This will make straight-edging and precise cornering much easier.

■ Use weaker-strength paints, such as washes, for the larger areas, and solid metallics only for the smaller shapes. This will prevent the latter dominating your scheme.

■ To change the color of any shape just repaint with pale turquoise and redraw the shape. This prevents any of the previous color showing through, especially around the edge, and is essential when the top coat is a wash.

This subtle color transformation will have your visitors wondering if their eyes are quite right; however, rather than being disconcerting it is actually very soothing.

optical illusion

In order to create this blended effect, making a smooth transition from one color to another, make sure that the colors you choose sit next to each other on the color wheel (see page 22). Choose your two paint colors and make the perfect mid tone by mixing together equal amounts of each. The success of the effect depends on the speed of the blending while the paint is still wet. Therefore, working on short lengths of wall at a time is the easiest technique. You can facilitate successful blending by applying the wallpaper paste to the mixture and by slightly dampening the clean blending brush before use. If the paint does start to dry up before you have smoothed out the join, just paint on more of each color and try again.

Groundwork The wall surface must be completely smooth for this technique since any dents or cracks will interfere with the blending of the colors. New plaster walls are perfect, or walls hung with heavy duty lining paper. This effect will not tolerate the smallest amount of unevenness. Prepare the surface accordingly, following the instructions on pages 18–19.

1 Marking up Measure the height of the wall starting from the floor and divide it into three sections. Draw horizontal lines across the wall using a ruler and carpenter's level, to act as a guideline for the painted bands.

MATERIALS AND TOOLS

- Turquoise matte latex paint
- Lime green matte latex paint
- Wallpaper paste
- Five 3″ (75mm) paintbrushes
- Two paint pails
- Tape measure
- Ruler
- Pencil
- Carpenter's level

2

3

2 The first band
Apply turquoise matte latex paint to the bottom band, cutting in roughly up to the guideline.

3 The central band
To mix a perfect middle tone for the central band, pour equal amounts of turquoise matte latex paint and lime green matte latex paint into a paint pail and mix together thoroughly. Paint in the middle band using this tone. Leave a very small gap between the middle and lower bands of color.

4 **Blending** Mix together equal amounts of turquoise matte latex paint and wallpaper paste in a paint pail. Apply a generous amount of the mixture to the gap between the central and lower bands of color. With a clean, slightly dampened paintbrush, run along this line blending the wash upward into the still wet paint of both bands. Add more of the wash mixture if needed and continue to blend until the lines have been completely softened.

5 **The top band** Paint in the lime green along the top band, leaving a small gap between the central and top bands of color. Now mix together equal amounts of the blended middle color and wallpaper paste in a clean paint pail. Apply a generous amount of wash along the join. Take a clean, slightly damp paintbrush and use it to blend the color upward and downward until the lines have completely softened.

Trade secrets

■ Do one section of the wall at a time, running over the corners. When dry, the corner that runs over to the next piece of wall should act as a guide for the color graduation, blending back over the last in order to ensure a consistent run. Slight variations will occur but should be kept to a minimum.

Using the most basic of tools, you can achieve a finish that has depth without being intrusive. The light colors chosen reflect the lightness of touch that is needed to sponge successfully.

simple sponging

The marks made using a sponge are quite crude and will vary in size and shape according to the type of sponge used. A natural sea sponge is fine in texture so will produce small, condensed prints. A large synthetic sponge needs to have holes pinched out of it to create a surface that will make suitable marks.

If a light color is layered over a darker shade, the overall effect will be soft and have depth, without the need to perfect each layer, as seen here. When using the opposite combination, the final layer must be quite even and applied with a consistent pressure.

Groundwork This technique involves laying on undiluted paint in a printed, mottled way, so will serve to disguise almost any flaws in the surface. Therefore only the minimum amount of preparation is needed before painting can begin. Prepare the surface accordingly, following the instructions on pages 18–19.

1

1 Preparing the sponge
Holding the sponge firmly in one hand, pinch out small chunks from around the edges and across the flat surface until the whole area is pitted.

MATERIALS AND TOOLS

- Aqua matte latex paint
- Pale aqua matte latex paint
- Large synthetic sponge
- Roller tray

2 Sponging Pour some aqua matte latex paint into a roller tray. Press the pitted sponge surface into the paint, then dab it over the raised area of the tray to remove the excess paint. Dab the sponge onto the white base coat, then lift it clean away so as not to smear the print. When working with undiluted paint the texture can be built up slowly as joins won't be visible, so don't rush. To work into the corners, tear off a small chunk of sponge and use it to dab into the recesses.

3 Finishing the first layer Continue sponging all across the wall until the surface is well covered but the white base coat is still visible through the prints. This layer will look quite strong and crude, due to the stark color difference, but this will be greatly softened when the next tone is applied. Leave the wall to dry thoroughly. Wash out the sponge before the paint dries on it.

4 The second layer Pour some pale aqua matte latex paint into a clean roller tray. Press the pitted sponge surface into the paint and remove the excess by dabbing it on the flat area of the tray.

5 **More sponging** Dab the sponge onto the dry first layer following Step 2. Continue across the surface, evenly covering without obliterating the white base and the first sponged layer.

6 **Topping up** Stand back from the wall to judge the evenness of the effect and apply more paint where needed. Treat the edges and corners as before with a small chunk of sponge.

5

6

Trade secrets

- As with any broken color effect, this look can be neatened by painting the edges quite  solidly and blending the paint into the rest of the wall finish.

- Try always to keep a consistent amount of paint on the sponge and continually angle the print differently.

- Any area that looks too solid can be repaired by responging with the base coat, blending out the area, and repeating the top coat.

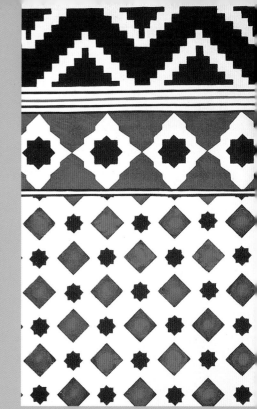

▶ Moorish tiles

This effect creates a powerful border in a stark white room. The effect requires three techniques: stenciling, stamping, and lining. Mark a border along the top of the wall using a carpenter's level and fill it in with solid dark blue matte latex paint. Leave to dry. Position a zigzag stencil over the border and paint in claret red (see pages 40–42). Use a lining brush to paint blue parallel lines below the stencil (see Step 6, page 32). Use deep green and dark blue to stencil the diamond border then line below this with dark blue. The larger area below the borders is stenciled with stars and stamped with turned squares (see Steps 5–7, pages 49–50). Once dry, coat the whole painted area with two coats of a high gloss varnish to imitate the high sheen of tiles.

◀ Two layer stipple

Subtle mottled washes of leaf green and khaki green have been gently stippled to soften the effect even further, and thus produce a calm atmosphere.

Nature's Greens

The green palette lends itself to modern styles as well as to more traditional patterns; several beautiful finishes using colors from the whole green spectrum are illustrated here giving you plenty of choice, with everything from faux rubber tiles to the distressed look.

▶ Rubber tiles

This easy trompe l'oeil effect aims to imitate the raised studs of industrial rubber tiles. Begin with a solid base coat of mid-green, then, when dry, measure out and mark a grid pattern using a 12" (300mm) square template. Use the end of a mini roller, with a 2" (50mm) diameter, as a stamp and apply the same mid-green to make circles centrally within the grid (see Steps 6–7, pages 49–50). Leave to dry. Cut a circle stencil with a diameter of 2½" (65mm), using a craft knife and thin card or acetate. Mix a lighter and darker shade of the mid-green by adding a little white to lighten it and black to darken it. Position the stencil over each stamped circle and brush dark green on one half of the circle and light green on the other half.

▶ Horizontal stripes

These horizontal bands of varying widths use six different tones from turquoise to lime green. The palest color is used as the solid base color since the darker colors will easily cover it and achieve a solid band in one coat. The stripes are applied with paint pads of varying sizes—1″ (25mm), 3″ (75mm), 4″ (100mm), and 8″ (200mm). Make a plan beforehand as to the size and color of each band, then draw the lines around the room using a carpenter's level and a pencil, taking the initial measurements from the floor or ceiling on each wall. Use the various widths of paint pads to apply the stripes, using the five shades of blue-green to green. Keep the darker tones for the narrower lines so that they don't become too overwhelming.

▲ Layered frottage

Washes of deep turquoise and bright green have been applied in layers and then treated with the frottage technique to create a textured look to the walls and ceiling.

▶ Leaf stamping

A stamp is an exact print of any object used. Therefore, many different tools can be tried. Here a leaf has been pressed until dry. Paint is lightly rollered onto the back of the dry leaf, over the raised veins to produce the best print. The leaf is pressed to the surface to make a skeletal print. To keep the whole effect within a natural context, a warm solid cream was used as the base color with a sage green used for the stamping. The positioning and spacing are kept random, and the angle of the print is constantly changed to imitate the look of falling leaves.

◀ Resist distressing

This effect is somewhere between a distressed look and a flaked paint finish. Candle wax is used as a resist between layers of differing tones of blue-green paint (see page 52), with a final layer of dry brushing (see Step 4, page 68). Rub the candle wax onto the surface in long strokes to imitate wood grain. Paint over the wax and, when the paint is dry, use a paint scraper over the waxed areas to scrape back the paint. Dry brush over the top by dipping the tips of the brush into the lightest blue-green, scrape off the excess, and drag the brush over the surface in the same direction as before to lessen the strength of the effect. The heavier the candle wax and the more contrasting the colors, the heavier the effect will be.

▶ Graded panel

Grading color (see pages 98–101) in a narrow area is far easier than grading a long run, so restricting the effect to thin, long bands around a room is the easiest approach. This will not only stop the look becoming too overpowering, but also make a good feature against a flat white base color. Draw long rectangles of equal width and height around the room, then mask off the shapes with low-tack masking tape. Dilute a strong green matte latex paint and a mid gray-blue in separate paint pails, with a ratio of 3 parts paint to 1 part wallpaper paste. Starting at the bottom of the panel, brush on the green, then, halfway up, start adding some blue, blending as you go until you finally end up with only blue at the top.

▶ Soft colorwash

This soft, broken color work is easily achieved using a wash and a large brush. The overall subtle effect is due to the color choices of solid white for the base coat and a gentle blue-gray for the top wash. Mix together equal amounts of blue-gray matte latex paint and water or wallpaper paste. Apply the wash to the wall using a large brush in random directions, keeping the strokes quite broad (see Steps 1–4, pages 44–47).

brown · gray · mahogany

Colors that you can mix and match, when fashion and your mood call out for something new, are the perfect choice for today's interiors. Sophisticated, pale tones of gray and brown are now *de rigueur* as an easy backdrop for the modern home, and using them is the perfect way to bring your home up to date without being too bold.

Interior design has gone crazy for fabrics such as wool, linen, and fake fur, which are chosen for the fullness of their texture. The paint colors that work best with these are creamy taupes such as mushroom, natural browns like mahogany, and washed-out soft grays, because they echo the colors of these fabrics. Using this palette of colors with stylish paint effect techniques will create sophisticated interiors that will last for years to come.

This palette sits perfectly with all natural fabrics and furnishings, particularly dark wood furniture, but is adaptable enough for the room elements to be changed without repainting the walls.

The power of paint effects is clearly illustrated in this project, where molded wooden paneling suddenly appears on what was once a flat white wall, using only household paint and brushes.

faux fancies

This simple trompe l'oeil effect imitates wooden paneling by treating the area as if it actually was real paneling. Consider how panel pieces would be cut and imitate this on the lower part of the wall. Treat the dado rail, door frame, and baseboard as part of the whole by dragging the same wash over the same base coat.

The color choice here is based on old oak and uses very flat tones of brown. Different woods have different tones so using a real piece of wood as the source of your color decisions will help the final look become more believable.

Groundwork The whole wall must be in very good condition to ensure this effect's success. Dragging and lining are used to create the wood panel effect, both of which need to be carried out on flat, smooth surfaces. Any obvious dents or cracks will ruin the lines, which need to be as straight as possible for the effect to work. Therefore, any old plaster should be lined and primed before this technique is tried. Prepare the surface accordingly, following the instructions on pages 18–19.

1 **The base coat** Apply two coats of pale beige matte latex paint to the whole wall area and leave to dry. Mask off the upper area of the wall, above the dado rail. If your room does not have a dado rail, these moldings can be bought from a hardware store and should be fixed about 30–36″ (75–900mm) above the floor.

MATERIALS AND TOOLS

- Pale beige matte latex paint
- Nut brown matte latex paint
- Large paintbrush
- 2″ (50mm) paintbrush
- Dragging brush
- Small fitch brush
- Paint pail
- Ruler
- Pencil
- Carpenter's level

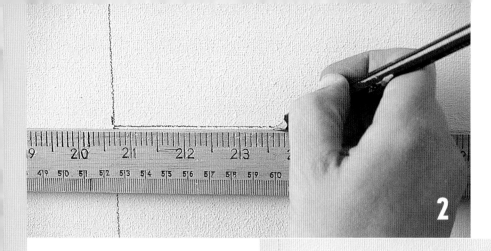

2 **Marking the panels** Measure and draw the paneling to a size that is in proportion to the length of the wall, and considering that the average dado rail is no higher than 36″. Use a carpenter's level to ensure your lines are perfectly straight.

3 **Masking** Mask off the horizontal side panels above and below the central square. The first parts of the panel to be painted are the vertical elements, which are filled in with vertical brush strokes. The horizontal elements, to be filled using horizontal brush strokes, are painted later.

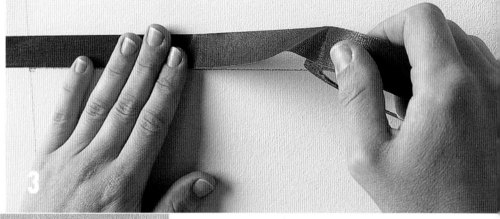

4 **The wash** Mix equal amounts of nut brown matte latex paint and water in a paint pail. Dip a clean 2″ (50mm) paintbrush into the diluted paint and scrape off the excess on the rim of the pail. Brush the paint vertically over one strut at a time.

5 **Dragging** Hold a dragging brush in one hand and place your other hand near the tip of the bristles— this will help you control the brush. Immediately pull the brush down through the wet paint, trying to keep the line as straight as possible. Run over the paint again while it is still wet if the drag isn't straight enough. Brush on the next section of paint and drag as before. When all the surrounding panels have been painted and dragged, go back to the central panels and paint and drag these in the same way. Remove the masking tape and leave to dry.

6 Working horizontally Mask off the vertical panels where they meet the horizontal panels. Use the same nut brown wash to fill in the horizontal panels, brushing the wash on using horizontal brush strokes then dragging through the wet paint in the same direction. Remove the masking tape and leave to dry. Paint the wash over the dado rail in long sweeping strokes.

7 Adding shadows Using a small fitch brush and the same nut brown wash, paint a brush-width band within the outline of the central square to act as a shadow line, as if the areas around it are raised.

Trade secrets

■ For a more professional look, use a graining comb over the wet paint, then lightly drag over either side of the heart grain created. When this surface has begun to dry a little, a softening brush can be lightly pulled along the grain to soften the effect for a natural look.

■ It can be helpful to hang a plumbline at intervals while you drag, to work as a guide to keep the effect straight.

This finish will bring your home right up to date, without requiring you to be too bold; and the look is fun and creative, while retaining an element of sophistication.

matte and gloss

A stunning look can be achieved by making a feature of the difference between flat matte color and a gloss finish. When matte latex paint is varnished it deepens the appearance of the color, which is further enhanced by the gloss finish. When the light catches the wall this checked pattern becomes more obvious, creating almost a self-patterned effect without the shapes being too dominating. Any shapes can be drawn, stamped, or stenciled, resulting in an endless list of possibilities easily created with the least amount of experience or expertise. The only disadvantage is that the varnished areas will need to be sanded in the future when you are ready for a change of scene.

Painting the base coat over your pencil lines is a good trick for making the marks faint while still visible enough to act as guidelines. They may initially appear to vanish, but will become more visible as the paint dries.

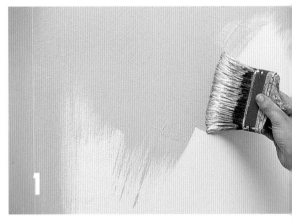

1 The base coat Apply two coats of taupe matte latex paint over the whole wall area and leave to dry.

Groundwork This overall effect relies on the use of flat matte color, which enhances dents or cracks, but also gloss varnish, which positively illuminates them. Therefore the surface of the walls must be completely flat and flawless. It is best to work on newly plastered walls or walls that have been hung with heavy duty lining paper. Prepare the surface accordingly, following the instructions on pages 18–19.

| **MATERIALS AND TOOLS** | ■ Taupe matte latex paint
■ High gloss acrylic varnish
■ Large paintbrush | ■ I″ (25mm) paintbrush
■ Flat, square artist's brush
■ Tape measure
■ Pencil | ■ Ruler
■ Carpenter's level |

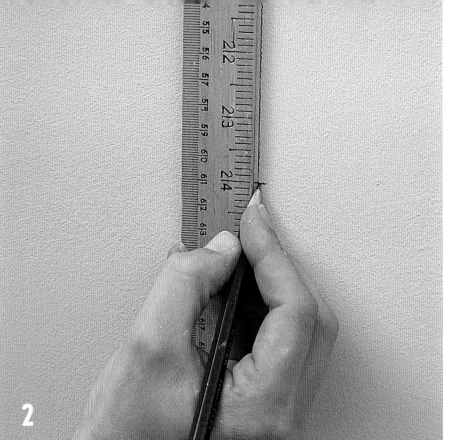

2 Verticals Decide on the size of the squares: these can be adjusted to fit the length or height of the room. Use a ruler to draw out all the vertical lines. Use a carpenter's level to make sure your lines are straight.

3 Horizontals Now use a ruler to draw out all the horizontal lines, and check them with a carpenter's level.

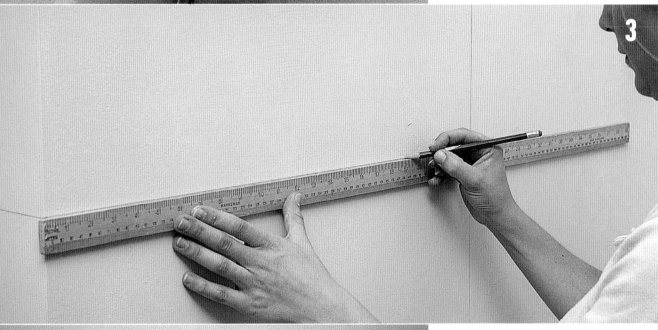

4 Covering the lines Take a little base color on a brush and lightly paint over the pencil lines. As the paint dries the lines will still be visible close up, but will be disguised by the varnish coat later. Leave to dry.

5 **Varnishing** Paint every other square with the high gloss varnish, using a 1″ (25mm) paintbrush and running as near to the corner as possible, and close to the pencil lines.

5

6

6 **Sharp edges** Use a flat, square artist's brush to apply the varnish right into the corners and along the lines. Two coats of varnish may be needed for a full glossy finish.

Trade secrets

■ This effect looks best when the wall is covered with full squares, rather than half squares at the baseboard or ceiling, for example. So work out the perfect size by dividing the height of the room. The square widths can still be worked around bends and in and out of corners.

◀ Suede effect

A soft suede effect (see pages 26–29) in warm beige complements the light wooden furniture of this entrance hall. In public areas, neutral tones are sensible as they are easy on the eye and very welcoming.

Earthy Tones

The rich colors of the earth and the soft subtle tones of gray suit soft, repeat paint effects rather than large-scale individual designs. Frottage, dragging, and sponging are all ideal techniques for this palette, but if you did desire something slightly more powerful then you could always try the leather look.

▶ Rag rolling

This technique mimics the look of folded fabric by pressing a scrunched up cloth into a wet wash. For a natural fabric feel, while keeping the effect quite strong, dilute a mid-taupe matte latex paint with an equal amount of water. Over a solid white base coat, roughly paint on the wash then rag it (see Steps 1–3, pages 26–27). Using different types and thicknesses of cloth creates variations in the print. Here, a chamois leather was used: once it is soaked the print will remain constant and the cloth is easy to handle. Use a paler shade over a darker one for a soft effect, while a darker tone over a light base will create a sharp finish, as here.

▲ Light and airy

The simplicity of sponging makes it the ideal technique for large expanses of walls. Also, when used in light tones, such as this delicate gray, it is not an overpowering effect, yet it is far more interesting than flat color.

◄ Light clouding

A soft mottled colorwash is created using one layer of diluted paint applied with a synthetic sponge. Start with a solid white base coat then mix together equal amounts of pale taupe matte latex paint and water or wallpaper paste. Dip the sponge in the wash and use a circular motion to apply it to the wall, then buff off any obvious smears or marks (see Step 1, page 30). Keep the base and top color similar if the effect is to be kept light and subtle, for a dusty finish use a light tone over a dark solid one.

VARIATIONS

► **Layered sponging**

This is a simple technique that layers undiluted paint in varying shades, relying on the sponge to make the marks (see pages 102–105). It can be quite a strong effect since the print from a sponge is dense, so carefully choose your tones, keeping them quite similar. Sponge warm gray over a solid white base coat, without totally covering the base. Then layer a lighter gray over the top, again leaving a little of the warm gray and white still visible. A different effect is created depending on the type of sponge used. A natural sponge is tighter in form so gives a more condensed effect. The alternative is to pinch chunks out of a synthetic sponge which results in a more open print, as illustrated here.

◄ **Leather look**

This effect relies on an initial buildup of a stippled texture, that is then painted over and rubbed back for emphasis. Paint on a very thick base coat of solid terra-cotta matte latex paint. Wait until the paint goes tacky, then stipple it using a broad brush in a pouncing motion. Leave to dry. This should leave an obviously pitted surface, but if the texture isn't thick enough, repeat the process until it feels rough to the touch. Paint a rich brown color over the top, then rub it back with a damp cloth before the paint has dried, removing the color from the raised areas, ensuring the effect remains quite even.

◄ Mottled colorwash

Using a warm beige over white with a two-layer
colorwash technique (see pages 62–65) creates an overall
mottled effect. Keeping the wash quite thin, about one
part matte latex paint to two parts water or wallpaper
paste, produces a subtle effect, especially when the second
layer disguises any joins or uneven application marks. The
white base is not close in tone to the top coat so brush
marks are obvious. The more extreme the tonal
difference in the two colors, the greater the effect will be.

► Plastic frottage

A plastic bag is used to create this sharp finish. Mix together 1
part taupe matte latex paint and 3 parts water. Brush the wash
randomly over the surface. Lightly scrunch up a plastic bag and
lay it over the still-wet wash. Lift it clean away to leave an exact
print of the folds of the plastic. Because the bag is non-porous,
none of the paint is absorbed, so crisp marks are made in the
wash. As the print is quite sharp and one-dimensional, a second
layer of the same wash can be applied to create depth and
soften any obvious marks. You can also vary the effect by
experimenting with different weights of plastic.

◄ Two-directional dragging

The dragging technique (see Steps 4 and 5, page
78) is worked in two opposite directions to create
a woven fabric effect. For a light feel a warm gray
is dragged over a solid white base coat. The
lengths must be dragged in a single stroke, so the
technique is limited to sections of a wall no higher
than standing height, such as in panels or below a
dado rail. Mix together equal amounts of pale gray
matte latex paint and water or wallpaper paste.
Brush the wash on in long sections, then drag the
still-wet wash with a dragging brush. Once all the
verticals have been completed, repeat the process
running in a horizontal direction.

VARIATIONS

Resource Directory

U.S.A.:

Absolute Coatings Inc.
38 Portman Road
New Rochelle, NY 10081
Tel (914) 636-0700
Fax (914) 636-0822
www.lastnlast.com

Adele Bishop
5575 N Services Road
Burlington, ON L7L 6M1
Tel (905) 319-0051
Fax (905) 319-0676
www.adelebishop.com

Albert Constantine & Sons 2050
Eastchester Road
Bronx, NY 10461
Toll-Free 1-800-223-8087
Outside U.S. (718) 792-2110
Toll-Free Fax 1-800-253-9663
www.constantines.com
(Also in Florida)

Artisan Supply Co.
5910 Arsenal
St. Louis, MO 63139
Tel (314) 645-4795
E-mail: fauxtools@aol.com
www.members.aol.com/fauxtools

Bayside Paint Company
3603 Camino Del Rio West
San Diego, CA 92110
Tel (619) 487-6006
Fax (619) 688-0082
www.baysidepaintcompany.com

Best Liebco Corporation
1201 Jackson Street
Philadelphia, PA 19148
Toll-Free 1-800-523-9095
Fax (215) 463-0988
E-mail: bestliebco@aol.com

Blue Ribbon Stencils
26 S Horton Street
Dayton, OH 45403
Tel (937) 254-2319
www.blueribbonstencils.com

Designer Stencils
c/o The Designer Shoppe, Inc.
3634 Silverside Road
Wilmington, DL 19810
Toll-Free 1-800-822-7836
Tel (302) 475-5663
Fax (302) 477-0170
www.designerstencils.com

Fine Paints of Europe
PO Box 419, Route 4 West
Woodstock, VT 05091
Toll-Free 1-800-332-1556
Fax (802) 457-1740
www.fine-paints.com

Firenze Enterprises, Inc.
12976 SW 132 Avenue
Miami, FL 33186
Tel (305) 232-0233
Fax (305) 232-3191
www.rivesto-marmorino.com

Frog Tool Company Ltd.
2169 IL Route 26
Dixon, IL 61021
Tel (815) 288-3811
Fax (815) 288-3919

Golden Artist Colors, Inc.
188 Bell Road
New Berlin, NY 13411-9527
Toll-Free 1-888-397-2468
Fax (607) 847-6767
www.goldenpaints.com

Kremer Pigments Inc.
228 Elizabeth Street
New York, NY 10012
Toll-Free 1-800-995-5501
Fax (212) 219-2394
www.kremer-pigmente.de

L.A. Stencilworks
16115 Vanowen Street
Van Nuys, CA 91406
Toll-Free 1-877-989-0262
Tel (818) 989-0262
Fax (818) 989-0405
www.lastencilwork.com

The Mad Stencilist
PO Box 5497 Dept N
El Dorado Hills, CA 95762
Toll-Free 1-888-882-6232
Fax (916) 933-7873
www.madstencilist.com

The Old Fashioned Milk Paint Co.
436 Main Street
PO Box 222
Groton, MA 01450
Tel (978) 448-6336
Fax (978) 448-2754
Canada (416) 364-1393
www.milkpaint.com

Paint and Decorating Retailers Association
403 Axminister Drive
St. Louis, MO 63026-2941
Tel (636) 326-2636
Fax (636) 326-1823
www.pdra.org

Paint Effects
2426 Fillmore Street
San Francisco, CA 94115
Tel (415) 292-7780
Fax (415) 292-7782
www.painteffects.com

R&F Handmade Paints, Inc.
506 Broadway
Kingston, NY 12401
Toll-Free 1-800-206-8088
Fax (845) 331-3242
www.rfpaints.com

Sinopia LLC
229 Valencia Street
San Francisco, CA 94103
Tel (415) 621-2898
Fax (415) 621 2897
www.sinopia.com

The Sims Collection
24 Tower Crescent
Barrie, ON L4N 2V2
Tel (705) 725-0152
Fax (705) 725-8637
www.simsdesigns.com

U.K.:

All About Art
31 Sheen Road
Richmond, Surrey
TW1 1AD
Tel: 020 8948 1277/1704

Annie Sloan
Knutsford House
Park Street
Oxford OX20 1RW
Tel: 0870 601 0082

Askew paint Centre
103 Askew Road
London W12 9AS
Tel: 020 8743 6612

Atlantis Art Materials
146 Brick Lane
London E1 6RU
Tel: 020 7377 8855

Bell Creative Supplies
Unit 5, Haslemere Pinnacles Estate
Coldharbour Road
Harlow, Essex CM19 5SY
Tel: 01279 427 324
Fax: 01279 437 550
E-mail: BellCS@aol.com

C. Brewers
327 Putney Bridge Road
London SW15 2PG
Tel: 020 8788 9335
www.brewers.co.uk

Brodie & Middleton Ltd
68 Drury Lane
London WC2B 5SP
Tel: 020 7836 3289

Craig & Rose plc
172 Leith Walk
Edinburgh EH6 5EP
Tel: 0131 554 1131
E-mail:
Inquiries@craigandrose.com

Crown Berger Europe Ltd
P.O. Box 37
Crown House
Hollins Road, Darwen
Lancashire BB3 OBG
Tel: 0124 570 4951

Farrow & Ball Ltd
Uddens Trading Estate
Wimborne
Dorset BH21 7NL
Tel: 0120 287 6141
www.farrow-ball.co.uk

Green & Stone
259 King's Road
London SW3 5EL
Tel: 020 7352 0837
E-mail: greenandstone@enterprise.net

C. Harrison & Son
High Street. Fordingbridge
Hants SP6 1AS
Tel: 01425 652 376

Leyland Paint
Kaim Decorative Products
Haddersfield Road
Birstall, Batley
West Yorkshire WF17 9XA
Tel: 01924 354 400

Planet Paint
www.planetpaint.com

J H Ratcliffe & Co (Paints) Ltd
135a Linaker Road
Southport PR8 5DF
Tel: 0170 453 7999

Stencil Craft
115 Boldmere Rd.
Boldmere,
Sutton Coldfield
B73 5TU
Tel: 0121 354 7070
www.stencil.co.uk

The Stencil Library
Stocksfield Hall
Stocksfield, Northumberland
NE43 7TN
Tel: 01661 944944
E-mail: sales@stencil-library.com

AUSTRALIA:

Porter's Original Paints
Sydney, Australia
Tel: 61 818 623 9394
Fax: 61 818 623 9210
www.porters.com.au

Index

A

acrylic glaze, as binder 20
acrylic paint 17
acrylic varnish, as binder 20
antique effects:
    using candle wax and petroleum jelly 52
    using woodstain 37
atmosphere 8, 9

B

basket weave 53
bathroom, color for 23
bedroom, patterned effect 9
binders 20
blending 98–101
blue:
    designs using 74–91
    effect on mood 8
borders:
    checked 91
    geometric 36
    stenciled 55
brown, designs using 110–23
brushes:
    cleaning 13
    coachliner 32
    dragging 12
    lining 12, 32
    paint 10–11
    softening 12
    specialty 12–13
    stencil 12
    stippling 12
    swordliner 12

C

candle wax 52, 108
carpenter's level 14
ceiling, giving effect of height to 23
chamois leather 15
checks:
    border of 91
    matte and gloss 116–19
chenille effect 73
claret, designs using 56–73

clay effect 54
cleaning brushes 13
cloudy sky effect 88
coachliners 32
color 22–3
    broken 23
    effect of light on 8
    effects of 22–3
    layering 21
color wheel 22
colorwash 17, 20
    as base for patterns 55
    clay effect 54
    covering capacity 21
    effects using 20
    making and using 20–1
    mottled 121, 123
    multi-toned 44–7
    over metallic paint 91
    pearlescent 37
    soft 109
    sponged 52, 88
    two-layer 62–5, 123
    undercoat 21
combs, rubber decorating 14
corners, painting 64
crackle glaze 34, 73
cracks, filling 18
craft knife 14
cream, designs using 24–37
cricket stripes 88

D

dado rails 7, 23
damask effect 70
decorating combs, rubber 14
découpage 70
denim design 90
distressed effects:
    dry brush 90
    resist:
        with flaked paint finish 108
        layered effect 52
dragging 76–8, 113
    two-directional 123
dragging brushes 12
drop cloths 10
dry brushing:
    distressed effect 90, 108

stone effect 30, 31
stripes 58–60
two-tone 66–9
dust masks 10

E

edges, sharp 73, 118
equipment:
    basic 10–11
    extras 14–15

F

fabrics:
    inspiration from 8, 9
    striped, effect of 58–61
    woven, effect of 123
feathery finishes 70, 80–3
features, designing around 8, 9
fillers 11
foam rubber 15
fossilstone marble 37
frottage:
    layered 107
    paper 72
    plastic 123

G

geometric designs:
    border 36
    in metallic paints 94–7
glaze:
    acrylic, as binder 20
    crackle 34, 73
    oil 85, 86
gloss paint, contrasting with matte 116–19
graded color 98–101, 109
gray, designs using 110–23
green, dark, designs using 92–109
grout float, using 85–6
grouting, effect of 32

H

holes, filling 18

I

impasto 17

K

knives, craft 14

L

ladders 10
latex paint 17, 21
leaf stamping 108
leather look 122
lemon, designs using 38–55
light, effect on color 8
light fittings, masking 19
lime, designs using 92–109
lime plaster 34
lining 76, 78
lining brushes 12, 32

M

magazines, ideas from 8
mahogany, designs using 110–23
marble, fossilstone 37
marbling 72
masking off 95
masking tape 11, 19
masks 10
masonry paint 17
masonry roller 15
matte paint, contrasting with gloss 116–19
metallic paint:
    geometric design 94–7
    wash over 91
milk paint 17
mirrors 7
"mist" coat 18
Moorish tile effect 106
mosaic, stamped 48–51
mother of pearl 37
mottling 91
mural, trompe l'oeil 88

N

natural shades 23
navy, designs using 74–91
neutral color schemes 24–37
New England look 76

O

off–white, designs using 24–37
oil glaze 85, 86
optical illusion 98–101
orange, designs using 38–55

P

pails, paint 11
paint pad 14, 34
paint pails 11
paint roller 11
paintbrushes 10–11
painting, order of working 19, 20
paints 16–17
    color for base and top coats 21
    layering colors 21
    types 17
    undiluted, effects using 21
paneling effect 112–15
paper frottage 72
patterns 9
    colorwash as base for 55
    stenciling 70, 71
    wallpaper 40–3
pearlescent wash 37
pencils 14
petroleum jelly 52
picture rails 23
planning 8–9
plaster:
    lime 34
    new, priming 18
    polished, effect of 84–7
plastic frottage 123
plumbline 14
polished plaster effect 84–7
powder paint 17
preparation 18–19
priming 18

R

rag rolling/ragging 26–8, 120
red, designs using 56–73
resist distressing:
    with flaked paint finish 108
    layered effect 52
roller fidget 54
rollers:
    masonry 15
    paint 11
rubber tile effect 106

S

safety 116
sandpaper 10
sandstone, effect of 30–3
scrapers 10
screwdrivers 10
Shaker look 76
sharp edges 73, 118
shelves 7
softening brushes 12
sponges:
    household 7
    natural 14, 102
    synthetic 7, 102
sponging 102–5, 121
    layered 122
    mottled sponged wash 52, 88
    stone effect 30–3
squares, sharp 73
stamp, making 50
stamping:
    leaf 108
    mosaic 48–51
stencil:
    making 40, 80
    preparing for use 41, 81
stencil brushes 12
stencil card 15
stenciling:
    border 55
    damask effect 71
    feathery finishes 70, 80–3
    wallpaper patterns 40–3
stippling 36, 55, 106
stippling brushes 12
stone (color), designs using 24–37
stone effect 30–3
stripes:
    cricket 88
    fabric look 58–61
    horizontal 107
    vertical 34
suede effects 26–9, 120
switches, masking 19
swordliner 12

T

tape measure 14
terra-cotta, designs using 56–73
texture:
    flattening 18–19
    use of 23

tiles:
    Moorish, effect of 106
    rubber, effect of 106
tones 22
tongue and groove effect 76–9
trompe l'oeil:
    drapes 35
    mural 88
    rubber tile effect 106
    wooden paneling 112–15
turquoise, designs using 92–109

U

undercoat:
    color 21
    for washes 21
universal tint 17

V

varnish, as binder 20
violet, designs using 74–91

W

wallpaper paste, as binder 20
wallpaper patterns 40–3
washes 17, 20
    as base for patterns 55
    clay effect 54
    covering capacity 21
    effects using 20
    making and using 20–1
    mottled 121, 123
    multi-toned 44–7
    over metallic paint 91
    pearlescent 37
    soft 109
    sponged 52, 88
    two-layer 62–5, 123
    undercoat 21
wood, for accessories 7
wooden paneling effect 112–15
woven fabric effect 123

Y

yellow ocher, designs using 38–55

Credits

Quarto would like to acknowledge and thank the following for supplying pictures reproduced in this book:

(key: l left, r right, c center, t top, b bottom)

p34tl Davies Keeling Trowbridge Ltd., p35 Neville Antony, p52tl Trevor Richards, p53t Davies Keeling Trowbridge Ltd., p70tl Trevor Richards, p71 Elizabeth Whiting & Associates, p88tl Davies Keeling Trowbridge Ltd., p89t Trevor Richards, p106tl Davies Keeling Trowbridge Ltd., p107t Elizabeth Whiting & Associates, p120tl Davies Keeling Trowbridge Ltd., p120–21tr Trevor Richards

All other photographs and illustrations are the copyright of Quarto.
While every effort has been made to credit contributors, Quarto would like to apologize should there have been any omissions or errors.